DEALS

DEALS

The Economic Structure of
Business Transactions

MICHAEL KLAUSNER

&

GUHAN SUBRAMANIAN

HARVARD UNIVERSITY PRESS
Cambridge, Massachusetts London, England
2024

LIBRARY OF CONGRESS CATALOGING-IN-PUBLICATION DATA

Names: Klausner, Michael, author. | Subramanian, Guhan, author.
Title: Deals: the economic structure of business transactions /
Michael Klausner and Guhan Subramanian.
Description: Cambridge, Massachusetts; London, England: Harvard University
Press, 2024. | Includes bibliographical references and index.
Identifiers: LCCN 2023031183 | ISBN 9780674495159 (cloth)
Subjects: LCSH: Negotiation in business. | Deals. | Contracts.
Classification: LCC HD58.6 .K574 2024 | DDC 658.4/052—dc23/eng/20230719
LC record available at https://lccn.loc.gov/2023031183

To Barbara, Jill, Greg, and Claire
and
To Sam and Mina

Contents

Preface

The origin of this book dates back about twenty-five years to the advent of a course with the same title: *Deals: The Economic Structure of Business Transactions*. Professors Ron Gilson, Victor Goldberg, and Dan Raff began teaching the course at Columbia Law School and Columbia Business School. Like this book, the course integrated economics and actual deals. The students would read economics and finance articles, and practitioners would present four deals to the class for the students to analyze. Three years later, I began teaching the course at Stanford Law School. I wrote up as case studies many of the deals that practitioners brought into the classroom. Over time, those case studies became the bulk of the materials included in the course—along with four or five new deals each year that practitioners would bring to class, and which would continue fueling the development of case studies. I made these case studies available to any other faculty who were interested in teaching Deals courses, and by now they have become fairly widely used. Guhan was among the first to use the materials at Harvard Law School and Harvard Business School. He also added his own case studies.

This book includes many of the case studies that Guhan and I have developed over the past two decades, so some of the deals go back many years. Fortunately, the relationship between deal terms and underlying economics is timeless. Deal terms may change over time, in response to changing economics or perhaps just fashion, but the logic of how deal terms respond to underlying economics remains constant.

We envision a few audiences for this book. One audience will be law and business students in courses on business transactions. The book can be used as a textbook. For faculty that want to teach from the book, we will be glad to provide additional case studies and problem sets to use in class.

The other audiences for the book are deal practitioners working in law, finance, and business. Practitioners with many years of experience usually have gained the knowledge and instincts required for their work. They may not need to understand the economics of adverse selection, moral hazard, and asset specificity, for example, to do their job well. They may have intuitions about when drag-along, tag-along, and put-call provisions fit a situation and when they do not. For them, a choice to learn the economics underlying their work might not be motivated by practical necessity so much as intellectual curiosity. But we hope it is useful to relatively junior practitioners—not as a "how to" book, which this certainly is not, but rather with the broader perspective of a "why to" book. Feedback from our students over the years has emphasized that taking the Deals course accelerated the process of accumulating knowledge and developing intuition relevant to deal-making. We wrote this book with that in mind.

Michael Klausner, September 2023

DEALS

INTRODUCTION

Business transactions are known for their complexity, voluminous documentation, and impenetrable legal language. The business-people involved often recoil at the stack of documents their lawyers produce, while their lawyers take pride in the completeness of their documentation and the "deal points" they score in negotiating what may appear to non-lawyers to be (and may actually be) minutiae.

The thesis of this book is that there is an underlying order to business transactions, and there are basic commonalities across transactions which, once understood, expose a degree of elegance and even simplicity in these monstrous masses of paper. Experienced businesspeople and lawyers involved in transactions have intuitions about the objectives of certain deal structures and terms. The analysis here brings rigor to those intuitions. It does so by using actual business transactions to illuminate the relationships between the economics underlying deals and the actual deal terms that address those challenges.

The objective of any deal is to carry out an exchange between parties. It could be a purchase of services or assets for cash, it could be a sale of securities, it could be a license of technology, it could be a combination of assets and services to create a business—the list could go on. An exchange occurs when both parties to a deal expect to be better off as a result. Of course, things may not work out that way, but the going-in expectation of each party must be that it will be better off as a result of the deal. Otherwise, why bother? In economic terms, deals are expected to increase *joint value* or equivalently, to create *joint surplus*—more aggregate value than the parties held before they entered into the deal.

The exchange can be simple or complex. But even in a deal that is complex overall, the exchange itself is often simple and may account for just a few lines of an agreement that spans dozens or hundreds of pages. Mergers and acquisitions are among the most common business transactions and often involve exchanges of billions of dollars in value, and hundreds of pages of documentation. The exchange, however, is typically quite simple. In an acquisition for cash, the acquiror buys all shares or assets of the selling corporation for an agreed-upon price. As one example (to which we will return in later chapters), Microsoft bought LinkedIn—or more accurately, all of LinkedIn's shares—for $196 per share. It did so by first creating a wholly-owned subsidiary, called Liberty Merger Sub, that it would then merge with LinkedIn, thereby making LinkedIn a wholly-owned subsidiary of Microsoft. Microsoft could have merged with LinkedIn directly with no merger sub involved, but the use of a merger sub provides certain advantages, including isolation of Microsoft from liabilities of LinkedIn that might crop up.

The terms in the merger agreement that accomplish this exchange are simple. The Microsoft-LinkedIn merger agreement provides that:

- each share of LinkedIn stock "will be cancelled and automatically converted into the right to receive" $196; and
- each share "of Merger Sub that is outstanding as of immediately prior to the Effective Time will be converted into one . . . share of common stock" of the surviving LinkedIn subsidiary.

That's the exchange. LinkedIn shareholders get cash for their shares, and Microsoft, the initial holder of Liberty Merger Sub shares, gets all the LinkedIn shares. Yet the Microsoft-LinkedIn merger agreement goes on for eighty-six pages, and points to many more pages of ancillary agreements and documentation. What is going on in those pages? That is the topic of this book—though with far more types of deals than mergers and acquisitions.

Whether in an acquisition or in any other sort of exchange, a consistent set of economic challenges must be addressed for a deal to be struck and the exchange to happen. These challenges form the framework of the book:

- Chapter 1 introduces the basic negotiation framework and the concept of bargaining power. This chapter is about the exchange, independent of the complexities the rest of the book incorporates into the analysis of a deal.
- Chapter 2 addresses challenges that parties often face in advance of a deal as a result of having less than complete information about the exchange they are considering. Parties may have asymmetric information about the value of the exchange, a situation in which *adverse selection* can occur. For example, a buyer often has less information about the asset it wants to buy than the seller has, in which case a seller may be hesitant to sell. The lack of information could instead be symmetrical—or it could be symmetrical with respect to some information and asymmetrical with respect to other information. In either situation, both parties will want to reduce any imbalance or incompleteness of information, as best they can, before entering into a deal.
- Chapter 3 introduces two mechanisms that can address such *ex ante* information challenges—earnouts and contingent value rights—which defer finalizing a price until after an exchange is made and more information is available. In light of how often ex ante information is incomplete, one might expect these mechanisms to be used frequently. In fact, because they can introduce more problems than they solve, they are not all that common.

· Chapter 4 continues our focus on information-related challenges. Here the question is whether the parties will be able to observe—and if necessary prove to a court—each other's performance after they begin implementing the deal. Is each keeping up its end of the bargain? If such *ex post* information is unavailable, a party may not be able to rely on legal enforcement of the deal as a means of either inducing performance or obtaining compensation for nonperformance. If this is recognized from the outset as a problem, concerns about *moral hazard* can impede a deal from being struck in the first place. A solution, as we will discuss, is to design incentives to induce performance—but that, too, entails economic challenges.

· Chapter 5 addresses deals in which at least one party needs to make an investment whose value depends on the actions of its counterparty—and where that dependency creates potential vulnerability. Economists refer to such investments as *asset-* or *relationship-specific*. One response is to protect those investments with long-term contracts.

· Chapter 6 continues the analysis of long-term contracts by investigating how those between buyers and sellers provide for adjustments in price and quantity as changes in the business environment occur. Without such adjustments, a long-term contract would be infeasible, but making the adjustment can be a complex and imperfect effort.

· Chapter 7 investigates *exit* mechanisms, particularly in settings where exit can result in a loss in value. Smart transaction design incorporates exit mechanisms that preserve value for both the party seeking to exit and the party that would prefer to remain.

· Finally, Chapter 8 analyzes the economics of how a contract is drafted, with particular focus on the use of specific *rules* versus broad *standards*. Rules can be difficult to write comprehensively, while standards can lead to uncertainty in performance and enforcement. Ideally, a contract will achieve an optimal tradeoff between these costs and benefits.

The economic concepts applied in this book are well understood by economists. Over the past thirty years, several economists have been awarded Nobel prizes for work related to the economics of contracts. Nonetheless, with this book we hope to make three contributions. First, by presenting a wide variety of deals from different settings—from biotech-pharma alliances to sports and entertainment financing, to supply contracts, and more—we highlight the commonalities among deals and the practical utility of the economic perspective.

Second, by illuminating the functions of deal terms and deal structures in this way, we show how they can be used to maximize the joint interests of the parties involved—and how things work out poorly when terms and structures are not used correctly.

And third, by grounding the concepts of contract economics in real business deals, we hope to broaden the awareness of those concepts to deal practitioners. The role of economic theorists is to develop mathematical models of economic relationships, using simplified examples to illustrate those relationships. We take the opposite and complementary approach of beginning with actual deals and analyzing them with economic concepts. Except where confidentiality requires anonymity, we identify the deals, which readers might choose to look into further.

1

THE BASIC NEGOTIATION MODEL
AND BARGAINING POWER

Deals are about creating value through an exchange. Even where there is the potential for a joint-value-creating exchange, however, a deal may not be struck. Much of this book is about how the economics underlying a potential deal determine whether it will be struck—for example, whether incomplete pre-contractual or post-contractual information may impede it. Before addressing those challenges, however, we address the roles of negotiation and bargaining power. Within the constraints of the underlying economics, negotiation determines whether a value-creating exchange will occur, and how the value created will be allocated between the parties.

The Zone of Possible Agreement

To illustrate the key concepts and vocabulary of the theory of negotiation, we start with an example taken from the classic book *Beyond Winning*, by Robert Mnookin, Scott Peppet, and Andrew Tulumello. The story begins with Sarah, who is about to go off to France for a year and wants to sell her car, a Honda Accord. She has found a dealership willing to pay $6,900 for it. She has also placed an ad asking $9,495.[1] The story's other character is Jim, who is shopping for a used car. He is considering another Accord that is not as old as Sarah's and that has lower mileage, selling for $11,500.

So, will Sarah and Jim strike a deal? In the seminal book *Getting To Yes*, Roger Fisher and Bill Ury coined the term BATNA, which stands for "best alternative to a negotiated agreement." It refers to a party's next best option other than the one being negotiated. In any negotiation, the price at which a party will buy or sell depends on his or her BATNA. So we begin with Sarah's and Jim's alternatives to striking a deal with each other. Sarah can sell her car to the dealer or wait to see what responses she gets to her ad. Jim's alternative is to buy the newer Accord for $11,500.

How do these alternatives translate into prices that Sarah and Jim would accept? They need to figure that out for themselves. Sarah must compare a sale to Jim today to the possibility of a response to her ad in the few days remaining before she leaves for France, and to a sale to the dealer at $6,900. How much would Jim have to pay for her to forego those options? This is her decision to make. The price she comes up with is called her *reservation price*. Let's say that price is $8,000.

What about Jim? How does he compare buying the newer Accord at $11,500 to buying Sarah's car? Again, only he can tell us. But getting into his head, let's assume he would be equally happy buying that car for $11,500 or buying Sarah's car for $9,000. That is, if Sarah demands a price above $9,000, he will opt for the newer car.

We now have enough information to take the next step. Sarah is willing to accept as little as $8,000, and Jim is willing to pay as much as $9,000. So, once again using the vocabulary of negotiations theory, there is a *zone of possible agreement*, or ZOPA, between $8,000 and $9,000. In economics this is called the contract zone. If Sarah and Jim arrive at a price in that zone, they will be collectively better off by $1,000, compared to the status quo of no deal, as of the time they are negotiating. The deal would create $1,000 in *joint value*.

But will Jim and Sarah make a deal and capture that value? Not necessarily. If Sarah proposes a price above $9,000, Jim may think there is no ZOPA between them, and end the conversation right there. The same is true if Jim makes an offer below $8,000. Sarah may perceive no ZOPA and walk away. Because Sarah wants the highest price she can get, and Jim wants the lowest price, their attempts at strategic bargaining may result in no deal. Even if they reach a point at which they are negotiating between $8,000 and $9,000, they may not settle on a price. Sarah may reject $8,200, even though it is above her reservation price, because she thinks she can get $8,500. Or Jim might reject $8,500, even though it is lower than his reservation price, because he senses Sarah will give up the car for $8,200. The two may give up and take their alternative deals without realizing they have a potential deal. Metaphorically speaking, the fact that there is a ZOPA means there is value sitting between them on the bargaining table. But they do not know it is there. Effective negotiators are good at identifying and capturing value when value exists.

Sources of Bargaining Power

This brings us to the topic of *bargaining power*, a term that is often thrown around in discussing deals. One side got a good deal, it is often said, because it had greater bargaining power or greater leverage than the other. What does that mean?

Despite the centrality of the bargaining power concept for negotiations, definitions vary. The most common definition of bargaining power, espoused in *Getting To Yes* and other important books in the negotiations field, is that a party's BATNA is the source of its bargaining power: the better your BATNA, the greater your bargaining power. Returning to Jim's and Sarah's deal, imagine that, before they strike a deal, another interested buyer responds to Sarah's ad with an offer of $8,500. With that improvement in her BATNA, Sarah will drive a harder bargain with Jim and accept no deal under that price. Her improved BATNA likely means she will

sell the car at a higher price than she would have without the intervening offer. The implication for negotiators is clear: if they want to
boost their bargaining power, they should seek to improve their
BATNA.

A variant on the BATNA analysis of bargaining power is cap-
tured in a familiar maxim: "whoever cares the least has power in the
negotiation." It is a reminder that one party's BATNA may be the
status quo—no deal at all. If that alternative is attractive to one side
and not the other, it has bargaining power. That party can comfort-
ably make bold demands at the bargaining table.

The economist Thomas Schelling identifies another source of
bargaining power in his classic book *The Strategy of Conflict*: para-
doxically, a bargaining advantage can be gained by deliberately tying
one's own hands. As Schelling puts it, in some settings it is possible
that "the power to constrain an adversary may depend on the power
to bind oneself; that, in bargaining, weakness is often strength, freedom
may be freedom to capitulate, and to burn bridges behind one may
suffice to undo an opponent."[2]

Schelling's insight is that bargaining power can come from the
ability to say "I'm sorry, but I really have no latitude to give any more
ground"—and having the other party believe this to be true. This
implies that, if the negotiator's hands are not in fact tied, it will be
advantageous to find a way to tie them, and very visibly make an
"irreversible sacrifice of freedom of choice." The famous—though
somewhat crazy—illustration of his point is in the context of the
game of "chicken": two cars come from opposite directions toward
a head-on collision, and the loser is the one who swerves to avoid
it. Obviously, if neither driver swerves, then both die in a fiery
wreck. The key to winning is to convince the other driver that you
won't swerve; if you can do this, then the other driver has no choice
but to swerve. Schelling points out that the most effective strategy
in this game is to unscrew your steering wheel and, in clear view of

your opponent, throw it out the window. Seeing this, the other driver has no choice but to let you win.

In the negotiation context, as Schelling explains, a buyer trying to negotiate a certain price has more power to succeed if the seller sees hard evidence that the buyer is not at liberty to accept a higher one. In his words, "if the buyer can accept an irrevocable commitment in a way that is unambiguously visible to the seller, he can squeeze the range of indeterminacy down to the point most favorable to him." There is a corollary, too: if bargaining power is achieved by cutting off one's own options, then both sides will try to do it, and the winner will be the side that can commit itself faster and more irrevocably to a position. Back in "chicken" terms, the game turns into a contest of who can throw their steering wheel out the window first.

Schelling allows that this tactic "is one that may or may not be available; whether the buyer can find an effective device for committing himself may depend on who he is, who the seller is, where they live, and a number of legal and institutional arrangements." And in truth, such extreme commitment strategies are rarely available in the real world. Yet there are less extreme, if less effective, ways for negotiators to shape the other side's perceptions of how much latitude they have to bargain. One way this is done is by feigning the existence of alternative offers. In the example with Sarah and Jim, let's say the intervening offer of $8,500 was subject to conditions that are unlikely to be met before Sarah leaves for France (for example, the buyer's ability to borrow some of the cash needed). If Sarah can nonetheless create the perception that her BATNA is an unconditional sale to someone else for $8,500, then she can credibly commit to taking nothing less than $8,500 from Jim, and Jim will pay at least that amount. Sarah "wins" the negotiation, because she gains at least 50 percent of the actual ZOPA, which is still the range between $8,000 and $9,000. Obviously, such a strategy is risky for Sarah since she doesn't actually know that Jim's reservation price is above $8,500, and if he walks away, she has spoiled a chance to do better than her real BATNA.

These sources of bargaining power are not inconsistent with one another. One's BATNA determines the limit that one will pay or accept. Improving one's BATNA will therefore enhance one's bargaining power. A party can do even better by convincing her counterparty that her BATNA is better than it actually is. And she can do even better if she can credibly bind herself to a yet more advantageous price—so long as that price is better than the other party's reservation price. There are practical limits, however, to these strategies. It may not be possible to convince the other side that one's BATNA is better than it actually is, and it might be even harder to credibly commit to a more advantageous deal.

We can also add another source of bargaining power, and one that, based on our observation of many real-world deals, may be the most important one of all: the advantage that comes with knowing the other side's BATNA. In the case of Sarah and Jim, if Sarah figures out with a high degree of confidence that Jim is willing to go as high as $9,000, she can claim exactly that as the price she requires, perhaps hinting at another prospective buyer in the wings willing to pay $8,900. If Jim believes her—a big "if"—he will pay $9,000, and Sarah will extract 90 percent of the ZOPA.

This additional source of bargaining power has different tactical implications from the others. Under the "BATNA is bargaining power" principle, a negotiator should work hard to come up with alternative deals. Under the "power to commit" principle, a negotiator should look for the real-world equivalent of a steering wheel to throw out the window. But under this third source of bargaining power, a negotiator should relentlessly probe the other side's BATNA. Again, these tactics are not mutually exclusive but can work together. Bluffing an attractive BATNA and credibly committing to a position are useful only if one stays within the

ZOPA—that is, if the deal is possible given the other side's reservation price.

In preparation for one recent negotiation, we saw a supplier establish a "clean team"—so-called because the team's members were otherwise not involved in the negotiation and therefore not contaminated with any particular biases. The team's job was to learn as much as possible about the alternatives available to the other side, a large existing customer. Any negotiator knows that it is important to put oneself in the other party's shoes and understand their perspective, but as a practical matter this can be hard to do. The clean team was an effort to get closer to a true understanding.

And it worked. The clean team concluded that, if no deal were made with their company, the customer's best alternative would be to buy from a certain competitor—but that doing so would force the customer to rework its manufacturing process, which would be costly. The value the clean team placed on this BATNA gave the supplier company greater confidence that it could insist on a particular price point, and in the end, granted it the greater share of the ZOPA.

Ethics and the Pursuit of Bargaining Power

We conclude our analysis of bargaining power with an observation on ethics. The question is whether it is ethical for Sarah to tell Jim that she has another offer at $8,500 when she does not. The conceptual starting point is *full, open, truthful exchange*, or FOTE.[3] FOTE is an important heuristic construct in negotiations, and at least superficially appealing to those who want to be ethical negotiators. When both negotiators employ FOTE, both truthfully reveal their reservation prices. Sarah divulges that she would take as little as $8,000, and Jim admits he would pay as high as $9,000. Once they have identified a ZOPA, the parties then split the surplus in some fair way. Typical FOTE models have the parties splitting the bargaining range in half, so that each side receives exactly half of the surplus. In this example, Sarah and Jim would agree on a price of $8,500, which would give each side the same $500 share of the bargaining surplus.

As appealing as this may sound, it is rarely a sensible way to approach a negotiation. The reason is that, in any negotiation, it is plainly in the best interest of each side to engage in strategic behavior rather than FOTE, so there is no reason to doubt that the other side will do so. If Sarah truthfully reveals her $8,000 reservation price, Jim will have an incentive to declare that his reservation price is, say, $8,400 and there is every reason to believe he will. Splitting the difference yields a deal at $8,200, which gives only 20 percent of the actual surplus to Sarah and 80 percent to Jim. Jim has gained more than half the surplus by departing from FOTE and engaging instead in strategic behavior. Of course, anticipating strategic behavior by Jim, Sarah also has an incentive to engage in strategic behavior—for example, by claiming a reservation price of $8,500 rather than $8,000.

It is generally acknowledged among negotiation scholars and practitioners that bluffing, posturing, shading the truth, and even lying are common tactics in negotiation. At one end of the spectrum lies FOTE. At the other end of the negotiating-style spectrum is what Richard Shell calls the "Poker School" of bargaining.[4] Just as one would not be surprised or shocked if someone lied in a game of poker, the Poker School regards negotiation as a game in which "deception is essential to effective play."[5] Context, of course, matters: the accepted negotiation norms that apply when haggling for a rug in the bazaar are different from those in negotiating family issues with one's spouse. As for the norms in business dealmaking, we simply note that full, open, and truthful disclosure is not expected with respect to parties' reservation prices. Bluffing about the general availability of alternative offers is the norm generally accepted in the context of business deals. Outright lies about other offers, however, are considered to be out of bounds.

Trading Across Terms

Thus far, we have provided a basic model of the negotiation process assuming a negotiation solely about price. This model is appropriate for a narrow—though important—set of cases, such as the used car exchange between Sarah and Jim. These price negotiations are sometimes called "fixed pie" or "zero sum" negotiations, because more for one side necessarily means less for the other.

In many negotiations, however, price is just one element of a more complex mix; other aspects of an exchange must also be agreed upon. The key to maximizing the value of such a deal is for negotiators to find trades among various elements. Effective negotiators move across issues, giving a little here to get a little there, with a commitment to the general principle that "nothing is decided until everything is decided." They seek deal terms that are valued differently by the parties at the table, and they trade across those terms. In addition to the economic terms, these other terms might be non-economic, qualitative, or even emotional. A seller of a family business, for example, might value an honorific title of "chairman emeritus" enough to give ground on another contentious point. Within this mix of elements, the price term generally remains open as a "lever" that can be adjusted up or down as needed to compensate for wins and losses on other issues. So, for example, a buyer might get greater flexibility to walk away between signing and closing an M&A deal in exchange for a higher price. These kinds of solutions are possible only if the parties can trade effectively across issues. Committing to the principle of "nothing is decided until everything is decided" helps them do so.

An alternative approach, more common among less experienced negotiators, is to negotiate one issue at a time. Analytically, each separate term becomes a fixed-pie negotiation, in which more for one side necessarily means less for the other. This issue-by-issue approach reduces the odds of reaching a deal, because an impasse on any one of these fixed-pie negotiations may crater the entire process.

An anecdote illustrates the power of "nothing is decided until everything is decided." An instructor who was teaching in a Harvard Business School executive education program projected that phrase on the classroom screen and began explaining its importance. One of the participants quickly left the room, returning some minutes later. After class he came to the front of the room to apologize for leaving so abruptly. He explained:

> Every year, I lead the negotiations with our labor union, to establish the terms of the contract for the upcoming year. Those negotiations are ongoing now. Every year we do the same thing: negotiate the new wage rate, whether it's a 2 percent increase or 3 percent increase or whatever, and then we lock it down and move on to the other issues. I had to leave class to go call my team and tell them: don't do that. Make sure "nothing is decided until everything is decided." Keep the wage rate open, and trade it off as needed against other issues.

A few weeks later, at the end of the course, when asked how the negotiation went, he had a positive update to share:

> It was great—for the first time, we could tell the union leader that we could give them certain "social issues," but we would have to take it back on the wage rate. So, we had a lever to pull that we never had before. Not only was it better for us, but we think it was better for them, too—because they got certain social issues that they would never have gotten in our old negotiation method.

While this prescription to keep the price term on the table is well accepted in the negotiation literature, and put into practice at least some of the time, it may not be implemented as often in certain types of deals, such as M&A transactions. To take an example from a Stanford executive education program, a team of experienced M&A lawyers performed a mock negotiation. They went through much of a typical merger agreement, bickering, scolding each other, saying they would "never allow a client to accept such a proposed term," and so forth. But once a term was (miraculously) agreed upon, they moved on to the next with no trading across terms. In a class discussion after the exercise, one of the lawyers acknowledged what lawyers generally report: that the price term can be adjusted in response to what is negotiated on other terms, but rarely is. This may be due to the fact that, very often, lawyers only begin negotiating M&A transaction documents after the price and other key terms have been set. But this way of organizing a negotiation violates the principle of "nothing is decided until everything is decided," and reduces the scope of gains that can be achieved.

2

EX ANTE INFORMATION CHALLENGES

The negotiation model described in Chapter 1 implicitly assumes that each party to a deal knows the value it places on the asset under negotiation. Often, however, this is not the case. Information about what is being exchanged may be imperfect. Typically, the seller is better informed about the value of what it is selling, but there are also situations in which the buyer has better information. Either way, there can be a problem of *asymmetric information*. It is also common for *both* the buyer and the seller to lack information regarding the value of the asset, so there may be *symmetric uncertainty*. Either asymmetric information or symmetric uncertainty can keep a value-increasing deal from being made. Parties to a deal, therefore, will not only want to improve their own information, they will also want to improve the other party's information. But there will be a degree of irreducible uncertainty due to unknown facts and future events. The parties must also negotiate how they will allocate the cost of that uncertainty.

Asymmetric Information

Information asymmetry can threaten even the simplest deals, like the used car transaction described in Chapter 1. In that situation, Sarah as the hopeful seller certainly knows more than Jim, the prospective buyer, about the car's quality. Let's assume the car has never been involved in an accident or shown signs of being defective.

Sarah has always taken it in for routine maintenance according to the manufacturer's recommendations, and parked it under a roof. She knows the car is in great shape and should fetch a price that reflects its value. Jim, however, is wary. Even if Sarah describes her loving care of the car, he might understandably discount her claims. Wouldn't anyone selling a used car give the same kind of report? Isn't there a chance that Sarah is saying she must sell the car because she is moving to France, when the real reason is that the car is no good? Racked by such doubts, Jim may make Sarah an offer too low for her to accept. And thus the chance could be lost for a deal that would be made easily if Jim had complete knowledge of the quality of Sarah's car. The asymmetry of information may yield an outcome that is unfortunate for both of them.

The problem of asymmetric information was first studied in the insurance context, where the term *adverse selection* was coined to describe what can happen when participants on one side of a market have information relevant to the value of an offering that the other side lacks.[1] This is the situation in the health insurance context, where potential policy buyers have more information related to their upcoming health care needs than an insurer does. People with the greatest health care needs are most likely to seek insurance—to "select" into the insurance market. As a result, the insurer faces a profile of applicants that will be more costly to insure than the population as a whole. This situation is "adverse" to the insurer's interest because the insurer does not know who selects into the market for this reason or how costly their care will be.

If the insurer could easily identify those high-risk applicants, it could price their policies in line with the expected costs of insuring them. But because the insurer cannot identify them, it rolls them into a larger group of policyholders, all of whom are charged a price sufficient to cover the expenses imposed by the high-cost members. Knowing that they, in effect, would be paying the health care costs of higher-risk policyholders, some healthy people select out and choose to go without insurance. Those remaining then skew the insured group even further into high-risk territory, with higher premiums needed to cover the insurer's costs. There will be some low-cost customers who choose to be insured because they place an especially high value on insuring themselves, but others will choose to be uninsured.

Legally mandated insurance, such as auto insurance, and mandatory employer-based health insurance are responses to this problem. They avoid adverse selection by requiring everyone, whether low- or high-risk, to join the pool of policyholders.

George Akerlof, in his famous article "The Market for 'Lemons,'" provides an economic model of adverse selection, with the used car market as an illustrative setting.[2] The motivation for the analysis is the question: Why does a new car lose such a substantial portion of its initial value the moment a buyer drives it off the lot? Akerlof offers an explanation unrelated to consumers' preference for new things or prestige. As he shows, the problem is that, as soon as a consumer has taken ownership of the car, the car moves from one market to a different market—a used-car market so shaped by information asymmetry that the worst-quality cars dictate the price that will be paid for any used car.

Akerlof starts by dividing the world of cars into new and used cars, and good and bad cars. In a new car transaction, there are randomly good and bad cars, but neither the buyer nor the seller has insight into whether a particular vehicle is a good or bad one. The price of a new car reflects the market's estimate of the average quality of a car model without reference to the specific vehicle in question. The used car market is different. The seller of a used car knows the car's prior driving history—whether a car is good or bad—while a potential buyer does not. The seller can share information about the car, but can the buyer believe it? The seller wants to make a sale for as high a price as possible, and therefore has an incentive to exaggerate the good, omit the bad, and perhaps lie outright. Unable to know the quality of a used car, the buyer implicitly discounts its value to account for the probability that it is of poor quality. Sellers of high-quality cars, therefore, are not able to sell their cars for their actual value, and many choose to keep their cars rather than sell them. Dropping the simplifying assumption of there being just two types of cars in the used car market, Akerlof shows that, in theory, better cars will be continuously taken off the market, and the average quality of cars will continuously deteriorate. The logical conclusion is that a market for used cars cannot exist—except perhaps for the very worst cars. Car owners who would like to sell their cars before they fully deteriorate, and individuals who would like to buy high-quality or medium-quality used cars will be unable to make deals with one another unless they can substantially reduce the information asymmetry, which of course real-world buyers and sellers find ways to do.

The negotiations literature has shown that adverse selection can be amplified in the bargaining process. Imagine that Sarah and Jim tentatively agree on a price of $8,500 for the car. Neither party knows this, but that price is exactly in the middle of their zone of possible agreement, with each party getting $500 of surplus relative to their BATNA. But now a thought crosses Jim's mind: Sarah knows more about the car than I do, so if she is willing to sell it for $8,500, it must not be worth that much. This phenomenon is known as *reactive devaluation*.[3] The seller's signal of receptivity to a deal provides new information that can lead the buyer rationally to reconsider its terms.

Of course, if taken to the extreme, reactive devaluation would be a complete barrier to any deal's getting done when there is information asymmetry between seller and buyer. The point is made succinctly in the movie *A Civil Action,* when John Travolta tries to persuade his co-counsel, William H. Macy, that they should not accept an $8 million settlement offer proffered by the defendant. "If they're willing to pay eight," he reasons, "then it's not enough, is it?"

Macy responds to Travolta: "Oh, that makes sense. That makes perfect sense. So, the only thing *you'll* accept is what *they're* not willing to give us. Listen to yourself!"[4] As an empirical matter, re-active devaluation does not occur in all deals, and as a prescriptive matter it shouldn't. If there is reason to believe that the buyer places a value on the asset higher than the seller's minimum, and the ZOPA is reasonably wide, a seller's acceptance of a deal does not imply that the deal is bad for the buyer.

Asymmetric information is pervasive in business deals, which often involve valuation challenges more complicated than assessing the value of a car. Consider the sale of an entire company, where determining value requires information about its assets, liabilities, business prospects, potential future liabilities, and more. The seller of the business typically knows much of this information—or, if not, it can acquire the information more easily than the buyer can. The same is true when a business is selling equity to an investor. Similarly, in the debt market, a borrower has more information relevant to the risk of default than the lender has. Or consider the case of a biotech company that is developing a drug. It is seeking an arrangement with a pharmaceutical company whereby the latter finances the drug's development and then, if the drug receives regulatory approval, it handles manufacturing and distribution. Each side of this deal has knowledge the other lacks. While the biotech company may know more about the biology of the drug, the pharma company will know more about manufacturing costs and the competitive landscape. Depending on the context, information asymmetry can run in either direction.

Symmetric Uncertainty

There are also situations in which both parties lack information on some salient aspect of a deal. Imagine, for example, that Sarah herself has come into possession of the car because her elderly father has decided his driving days are over and signed the title over to her. If Sarah knows nothing about whether her father has had problems with the car, she and Jim are equally uninformed. Uncertainty regarding the quality of the car is symmetrical. In this situation, they may or may not reach a deal. Jim will discount the car as he would ordinarily, given the probability of badness he assigns to it, and Sarah, equally lacking information, will also discount the car's value to some degree, but their discounts may not be the same.

In a complex business deal, symmetric uncertainty on certain points can coexist with asymmetric information about others. In the sale of a large corporation with worldwide operations, a seller's management surely knows a lot about the business being sold, but there can still be important questions to which it does not have the answers. It may not know with certainty whether, somewhere in its far-flung operations, it is unwittingly violating someone else's intellectual property or violating local law. These are also matters of which the buyer is ignorant, so the two sides face symmetric uncertainty to a degree.

Where information about a possible exchange is incomplete, the parties must find ways to obtain sufficient information to move forward with a deal. And to the extent uncertainty is irreducible, they must come to an agreement on how they will allocate the cost of that uncertainty. As we will see, the process of negotiating that allocation can complicate how the parties provide information to each other.

Responses to Incomplete Information

In response to incomplete information, whether asymmetric information or symmetric uncertainty, parties must find ways to inform themselves—and each other, since, as noted above, an information advantage may not actually be advantageous. In some situations, information can be communicated directly, but in others, parties must devise indirect ways of conveying or obtaining information.

Signaling Hidden Information

Consider the hypothetical case of Analyst Research and Reports on the Web, Inc. (ARROW), a company that has an innovative product nearly ready to launch but is in desperate need of cash.[5] The company has built a database that includes tens of thousands of securities analyst reports and coupled it with an artificial intelligence tool capable of synthesizing information scattered across those reports, identifying patterns, and unlocking information not otherwise available. The product targets a market of investment managers and advisors, management consultants, accountants, corporate strategic planners, and product planners. This is an attractive proposition for all concerned. ARROW waits two weeks after a brokerage firm has distributed an analyst's report to its clients to post a report to its database, by which time the report will have lost much of its direct value. ARROW thus avoids taking a competitive position vis-à-vis the brokerage firms that produce the reports, and pays royalties to those firms. ARROW already has commitments from major brokerage firms to contribute several years of analyst reports for five thousand companies, which should be sufficient to launch the product. Feedback is good from a small group of users of the product's beta version.

Brian Benjamin, ARROW's founder and CEO, believes the company is on the brink of proving its technology and signing up a critical mass of clients—and then enjoying rapid growth and tremendous financial returns. Before that successful commercial launch can happen, however, there are some technical and marketing hurdles to clear. ARROW needs to prove that its technology can serve a very large number of users simultaneously. And it needs to execute an ambitious marketing blitz to attract the several thousand users that Benjamin figures must be in place within mere months to establish a base for exponential growth. Having met with many large corporate prospects, Benjamin is optimistic that ARROW will meet its sales goal. He also believes that the technological challenges can be met in six months. If it takes much longer, however, he fears that ARROW might miss its window of opportunity. A competitor with the same idea could make it to market and deny ARROW its market dominance. In short, ARROW is ready to make a final push toward becoming a fabulously successful business—but for that to happen it will need new funding fast.

Benjamin has been negotiating with ABC Ventures, a current investor in ARROW, to lead a new round of financing. The people at ABC are confident that, if ARROW can meet its short-term challenges, it will be successful. They hold Benjamin in high regard as a very capable computer scientist with key traits they like to see in an entrepreneur. But ABC is not thoroughly convinced that ARROW can both scale its technology and attract a critical mass of users in the six-month timeframe Benjamin is projecting.

ABC therefore has decided to make Benjamin two nonbinding offers from which he can select one as the basis of continued negotiation. Offer number one is for a $15 million investment at $2.50 per share. At ARROW's expected burn rate, this amount of cash will last about eighteen months—well past the point at which Benjamin expects ARROW to be cash-flow positive. Offer number two is for $6 million at $3.00 per share. This cash will keep the company going for roughly seven months, at which point, ARROW will need additional funding, even if it meets its immediate engineering and marketing goals.

Which should Benjamin accept? Offer number two is more attractive financially if things go well in the coming months and the goals are met. On the other hand, offer number one gives Benjamin a lot of leeway in case ARROW misses its engineering objective or its sales target. The choice might be difficult—but it could also have greater consequences than Benjamin realizes. If he chooses offer number one, we predict that ABC will cut its losses and walk away altogether. But if he chooses offer number two, ABC will move forward to sort out the details and quickly provide financing.

Why? By choosing offer number one, Benjamin would convey information to ABC regarding his lack of confidence that ARROW's challenges could be overcome within six months. Or at least ABC could reasonably interpret his choice this way. If Benjamin instead chose offer number two, he would signal confidence in his six-month projection. That signal would be backed up by the fact that, if he were wrong and ARROW failed to meet its six-month target, Benjamin would pay a high price. He would have no leeway, and his company would likely fail. The signal of choosing offer number two would thus credibly convey information regarding Benjamin's confidence.[6]

In this deal, ABC faces an asymmetry of information with Benjamin. It responds to that asymmetry by forcing Benjamin to convey his private information regarding ARROW's prospects. Benjamin will either convey confidence, or he won't. ABC will then respond to information it receives by either moving forward with a deal or not. Of course, Benjamin could convey the same information at the outset by asking for only six months of financing. Either way, a credible signal of Benjamin's confidence will be sent. In other situations, information is conveyed more directly, but it still must be conveyed credibly. There must be a cost to conveying false information.

Direct Disclosure of Information

The most straightforward way of addressing incomplete information is for the party in possession of the information simply to disclose it to the other.[7] The seller in a used car deal, for example, can compile maintenance and repair records to share with the potential buyer. In many types of transactions, such as corporate loans and corporate acquisitions, information is conveyed by page after page of *representations and warranties*, and accompanying disclosure schedules. When a company is acquired, for example, the seller's "reps and warranties" (or, even shorter, just "reps") and its disclosure schedules convey details regarding the business, assets, liabilities, and potential liabilities of the company being sold. The standard format provides reps subject to exceptions listed in the accompanying disclosure schedule. For example, a rep may state that "except as listed in the disclosure schedule, there is no litigation pending against the company." The disclosure schedule then lists all the pending litigation.

Reps and disclosure schedules are often voluminous and detailed. They typically include a statement that the company's financial statements were prepared in accordance with generally accepted accounting principles (GAAP in the US, usually IFRS elsewhere), and that they fairly present the company's financial position. The reps disclose the company's potential tax obligations, its contractual rights and obligations, its compliance with environmental laws, its pension liabilities, its ownership of intellectual property, whether it has any labor disputes, and many other matters that influence its value. The reps also include an attestation that the company's performance has not changed materially since its last financial statements.

Whether a buyer is negotiating to acquire a car or to take ownership of an entire business, however, that buyer must be able to rely on the seller's representations. In extreme cases of deception, of course, the managers of a selling business might face prosecution for criminal or civil fraud, but these situations are rare.

For a seller's reps to be credible, the seller must face a substantial cost if the information it conveys turns out to be false. When a privately held company is sold, this is accomplished by having the shareholders of the company indemnify the buyer against any losses stemming from a false representation. The seller typically gives the buyer a period of time after the acquisition to discover the problem and make a claim, and it often puts cash in escrow to cover claims that arise. The commitment to indemnify the buyer makes the seller's reps credible.

When a public company is sold, however, it is not feasible for a seller to indemnify the buyer. The sellers are dispersed public shareholders who are difficult to track down and who had nothing to do with making the representations in the first place. The primary mechanism that makes public company reps credible is the right of the buyer to walk away from the deal before closing, if it finds that a representation is false. In a public company sale, there is typically a period of a few months between the day the buyer and seller sign an acquisition agreement and the day the deal closes. The agreement provides that if, during that time, the buyer discovers a representation by the seller to be materially false, the buyer has the right to terminate the deal—to "walk." Between signing and closing, a buyer continues collecting information about the business it is about to purchase, and attempts specifically to verify what the seller has represented.

A buyer walking away from a deal is costly to the seller's management and shareholders. It sends a signal to the market that there is something wrong with the target company. What exactly that problem is might not be clear. The rep that the buyer finds to be false might itself be the deal-breaker, because the corrected information shows the company is not as good as the market thought it was. Or perhaps the discovery of a false rep just provides the buyer with a convenient, contractual excuse to walk away for an unrelated reason—maybe because it has developed serious qualms about something less tangible. Regardless, the market's response to a failed merger is ugly: the seller's share price falls and its managers, who have made the false rep, bear costs through their shareholdings, their stock-based compensation, and their reputations. Walk rights, therefore, have teeth.

The case of Fresenius's acquisition of Akorn illustrates the power of walk rights in an extreme form. In April 2017, Fresenius Kabi AG, a large German pharmaceutical company, agreed to acquire Akorn, Inc., a smaller pharma company based in the United States, for approximately $4.3 billion. Akorn made extensive representations in the acquisition agreement regarding its compliance with applicable regulatory requirements—a critical concern for the acquiror of any pharma company. In October 2017, before the deal closed, Fresenius received an anonymous letter that raised questions as to whether Akorn was indeed in regulatory compliance. Fresenius investigated these allegations and discovered serious data integrity problems at Akorn. In April 2018, Fresenius gave notice that it was terminating the merger agreement, claiming that the regulatory compliance representation was untrue and the noncompliance was material to the company's future profitability and present value.

Akorn took Fresenius to court, arguing that Fresenius had no right to terminate its agreement. But the Delaware Chancery Court disagreed and let Fresenius walk.[8] With this ruling, Akorn—which had already lost about 45 percent of its share value when Fresenius announced it was walking away from the deal—lost another 45 percent, for a total decline of 90 percent from its pre-deal value. And with its regulatory noncompliance now on public display, Akorn was damaged goods in the marketplace. In May 2020 it filed for bankruptcy.

In a sale of a company, the threat of individual liability can also play a role in providing assurance to buyers. When a private company is being sold, the acquiror may demand affirmation of a target company's representations by its controlling shareholder or shareholders, thereby exposing them to liability if a rep turns out to be false. In a sale of a public company, terms can be written into the acquisition agreement by which specified senior officers of the company stand to be held personally liable if they are found to have intentionally deceived the buyer.

Self-Help

Another way in which parties reduce information asymmetry is by collecting information themselves, often with the cooperation of their counterparty, through the process known as *due diligence*. In any deal, there is an initial period of investigation during which the buyer determines whether it is interested. In an acquisition, that period may begin with a tentative price proposed by the seller and a tentative expression of interest by the buyer, subject to due diligence. The initial period often ends with a nonbinding term sheet or letter of intent that sets a price and spells out other major points of the deal—all subject to the buyer's eventual agreement after further investigation.

Due diligence at the initial stage and throughout the dealmaking process is costly—and the more time-consuming and costly it is, the less likely the buyer is to engage in the process. Rather than incurring the cost, a buyer may lose interest in a deal, or may make a low offer that takes into account its minimal due diligence has been inadequate and its information is highly incomplete. Assuming the seller wants the deal to move forward on terms it will find attractive, it will try to make the buyer's due diligence as easy and productive as possible. At some point in the process, the two may also enter into a time-limited exclusivity agreement, which provides the buyer with some assurance that, if it invests in due diligence and is happy with what it finds, it will be able to go forward with the deal. Without an exclusivity agreement, the buyer might invest heavily in due diligence only to lose the deal to another party.

If the buyer and seller reach a preliminary agreement, they go on to negotiate and draft a full, definitive agreement, complete with the seller's representations and warranties. The buyer's due diligence continues, however, up until the time of closing. The buyer's right to walk—and hence, the seller's reps and warranties—work because of the buyer's continued due diligence. To walk, the buyer must discover that one or more of the seller's reps is untrue; and to induce the seller to take care in making truthful reps, the buyer must make it clear that due diligence efforts will continue.

A buyer engages in due diligence not only to validate information the seller has conveyed, but also because there is some information that a seller cannot credibly disclose. For example, while the seller of a business can represent that a list of contracts with customers and suppliers is complete, and it can disclose the terms of those contracts, the seller cannot effectively represent that its relationships with customers and suppliers are good, which of course can be important to the value of a business. The buyer will need to get that information itself by speaking with the parties with which the seller has contracted.

Outside the context of mergers and acquisitions, some deals rely more on due diligence than on a seller conveying information to a buyer. Some acquisitions of land are examples. The following case is loosely based on *Mattei v. Hopper*, a legal dispute from the 1950s that remains in many law school textbooks today, and featuring a legal issue that continues to be litigated today (though that issue is not the point of the story here).[9]

Peter Mattei was interested in buying an undeveloped tract of land on which to build a shopping center. But he did not want to buy the land unless he knew he could enter into a lease with an attractive anchor tenant on terms that suited his plans for the shopping center. He entered into a deal with Amelia Hopper, the owner of the land, under which he would pay an agreed upon price subject to the condition that he was free to walk away if, in his sole discretion, he determined that he could not enter into a suitable lease with an attractive anchor tenant. In effect, Mattei had a free option to buy the land. The term for this arrangement is a *free look*.

The free look allows a buyer to incur due diligence expense with assurance that it can buy the land at an agreed-upon price if the results of the due diligence justify doing so. But this assurance comes at a cost to the seller. The seller has to take the property off the market while the free look is in effect, and therefore loses the possibility of getting a better deal during that time. So, what does a seller get out of giving a buyer a free look? Some courts have concluded that the seller gets nothing in return for its commitment to the buyer. Based on this understanding, they have ruled that these agreements are not enforceable contracts. (To be enforceable, a contract must provide a benefit to both parties.) But this view of the free look reflects a misunderstanding of the economics of the deal. What a free look provides to a seller is a greater likelihood of selling its land for the agreed-upon price, or equivalently, the opportunity to sell the land at a price higher than it could without the free look. The free look gets the buyer and seller past an information hurdle that would otherwise result in a less valuable deal to the seller, or no deal at all. In effect, the seller is paying the buyer to collect the information it needs to justify the price the seller seeks.

The free look, however, raises a couple of issues. First, could the seller provide a buyer with the information he needs? If the buyer is concerned about groundwater pollution or soil content, perhaps it could. But there is no way for a seller to assure a buyer that it will be able to sign a lease with an attractive anchor tenant on attractive terms. This is something the buyer will have to determine for itself. It will have to actually negotiate a lease with a prospective tenant, and the only feasible way of doing that is to assure a would-be tenant that the buyer will close the deal on the land if they reach an agreement on the lease.

Second, why is the free look *free*? In a hot market, the cost of taking a property off the market could outweigh whatever gain would result from a sale following the free look. A fee can make up for the difference. In fact, in some real estate deals, the seller charges a fee for the look, which it waives if the buyer goes through with the purchase.

Third-Party Assurance

Parties to a deal may also rely on third parties to provide information. In a used car sale, a buyer may ask a mechanic to inspect the car. In business transactions, buyers and sellers commonly retain accountants, investment bankers, and lawyers to provide information upon which they rely. For example, a common third-party assurance on which buyers rely is an audit by an independent accountant. Legal opinions of seller's counsel are common, as well. These opinions can address the seller's title to assets it purports to own, the absence of contractual restrictions on sale, and other legal issues related to the consummation of the transaction and what the buyer will get when the deal is done.

Assuming no attempt at outright fraud, both buyer and seller have a mutual interest in engaging a third party whose credibility is well established. Third parties that are successful at credibly conveying information generally share three characteristics: they have expertise in their field; they are recognized as objective and impartial; and they have a reputation that they will put in jeopardy if the information they provide turns out to be untrue.

In some situations, a third-party assurance can be indirect but still highly effective. Consider the following "slate financing" deal between a prominent Hollywood producer and a group of hedge funds. The former proposed to produce a slate of fifteen yet-to-be-selected movies over five years, for which the latter would provide financing. Deals like this face a number of challenges, as will become clear with a closer look at this deal in Chapter 4. For our purposes here, note that one problem for the producer was to convince investors that they were dealing with someone with an exceptional ability to select good scripts and make good movies. Of course, the investors could see the movies the producer had produced in the past, but that would not be enough to show them a success rate. Perhaps there were many other projects that never made it to the screen. The producer could put the investors in touch with others in Hollywood who would provide glowing references, but such attestations would be of questionable credibility.

Instead, the producer built third-party assurance into the terms of the financing agreement. The agreement provided that, prior to closing, the producer must have in place an agreement with a major film studio to advertise and distribute all the films in the slate. Furthermore, that agreement would have to include commitments by the studio to distribute all movies in the slate to a specified minimum number of movie theaters, and to spend at least a specified amount on advertising.

This commitment would be costly for the studio. Roughly ninety percent of advertising expenses are incurred before a movie is released, so a great deal of money can be lost advertising a movie that turns out to be a dud. There are high opportunity costs, too, since there is a limit to the number of movies a studio can distribute at any time. Committing itself to this producer's full slate of movies would mean that the studio could not distribute other movies. And committing to a slate without knowing the content of the films would run the risk that some of those films would compete directly with other movies the studio would want to distribute. The studio would not agree to these terms unless, based on its prior experience, it truly expected good movies from this producer. The studio's commitment also ensured the investors that scarce theater spots would be available for the movies in the slate, but that assurance was a consequence of the studio having faith in the quality of the producer's movies.

Price Discovery via Auction

When it is the seller who is uncertain about the value of an asset, an alternative to investigating the value of the asset or seeking the assistance of a third party might be to put the asset up for auction. In effect, potential buyers will inform the seller of the asset's value via their bids. Auctions can be complicated, but where they work well, the seller can remain blissfully ignorant of the asset's value until competitive bidding provides the answer.[10] In economics terms, an auction can under certain conditions be an effective mechanism for price discovery.

Three factors that determine an auction's ability to perform this function include the cost of bidding, the extent to which potential bidders are informed regarding the value of the asset being sold, and the number of potential bidders that participate in the auction. Regarding the first, participating in an auction is not costless—it involves at least some investment in evaluating the asset up for sale and deciding how high to bid for it. If an asset is complex and difficult to value, potentially interested buyers may be deterred from taking part. A seller can often respond to this possibility by making whatever information it does have easily available to bidders, or by engaging an expert third party to attest to the asset's condition, authenticity, or other qualities. An auction needs enough bidders but not too many. Too few bidders can be problematic if those participating do not include parties that will potentially value the asset highly, that will become informed of its value, and that will have sufficient cash or financing to let the price reach the value of the asset. Too many bidders can also be a problem. The greater the number of bidders, the less likely any one bidder will be to succeed, which can deter bidders from participating. A seller can respond to this problem by screening and limiting the number of bidders permitted to make a bid.

Deal processes balance these competing concerns through a hybrid of negotiation and auction processes—what one of us has called "negotiauction" deal processes.[11] For example, a buyer trying to procure an information technology system might advertise a request for proposal, to which IT providers could respond with first-round indications of interest. Based on these indications of interest, the buyer might then winnow down the field of bidders to, say, two or three and engage in one-on-one intensive negotiations with each of them.

Agreeing to Wait and See

Finally, in some situations where parties face incomplete information and cannot agree on a price for an asset, they may agree to an initial payment at the time the asset changes hands, and then an additional payment or payments after it has been used for a period of time and its value has become clearer. Technology and trademark licenses typically take this approach. Rather than trying to predict the value that will be realized in the future and setting an upfront price, the licensee pays the licensor an ongoing royalty while the asset is used. The royalty is typically based on unit sales or on revenues generated from the sale of products that use the technology or trademark.

Similarly, in some corporate acquisitions, parties agree to an earnout or contingent value right (CVR)—mechanisms addressed in detail in Chapter 3. These provide that the buyer will make a payment to the seller based on post-acquisition metrics designed to measure the value of the acquired company over a period of time following the acquisition. As we will see, however, neither mechanism is as promising as it might appear at first glance.

When Uncertainty Is Irreducible

Ron Gilson, in a widely and rightfully acclaimed article, raised an interesting question: Given that sellers have a strong interest in informing buyers regarding the value of an asset being sold, why do lawyers negotiating corporate acquisitions spend so much time bickering over representations and warranties?[12] (Negotiating reps and warranties is a task generally delegated to the parties' lawyers.)

Shouldn't representations and warranties be worked out as a co-operative effort to provide the buyer with information it needs to justify paying the price the seller seeks? Gilson's analysis and our discussion above—now forty years later—suggests that it should be. But, as Gilson recognized, it is not. Negotiating representations and warranties is very adversarial. Why is that? Gilson did not offer an answer, except to suggest that the lawyers are "seduced by the prospect of combat."

Gilson's read on lawyers negotiating reps and warranties may well be correct—certainly with respect to some lawyers. But we offer an additional explanation. There are certain facts about a company that the seller does not know and cannot discover without inordinate time and effort. For example, buyers often seek a representation from a seller that neither the seller nor any other party is in breach of any material contract. The seller's lawyer may well respond that management of the seller does not know for sure whether this is true. The company has many material contracts with many parties around the world, and it is difficult to keep track of whether anyone is out of compliance. If the seller provides a representation, it bears a cost. If, in pursuing its due diligence, the buyer finds that the rep is untrue, the buyer can walk or, under the threat of walking, it can negotiate a better deal for itself. On the other hand, if the seller does not provide the rep, the buyer bears a cost. Noncompliance with a contract, by the seller or its counter-parties, may mean substantial costs in the future—to come into compliance, to get the other side to come into compliance, or to adapt in some other way. As a result, negotiating this rep—in contrast to those about which the seller is certain—is a matter of allocating the cost of the unknown. Hence, it is not an inherently cooperative endeavor.

To make matters worse, the seller may bluff and feign resistance to giving a rep that it could give costlessly, and argue that the buyer should concede something in return. The contentiousness of negotiating the costly reps thus spills over into the negotiation of the costless, or low-cost, reps. Thus, negotiation of reps and warranties is simultaneously about information transfer and cost allocation. This dual role creates a complication that practitioners intuitively understand, but that has not been fully conceptualized. The implication is that we should not expect the negotiation of reps and warranties to be entirely cooperative.

Some sources of irreducible uncertainty are external to the business or other asset being exchanged, but will predictably affect its value. Examples include events such as natural disasters and changes in the economy, an industry, or technology that occur before a deal is fully performed. In a corporate acquisition, the relevant time period is between the time the acquisition agreement is signed and the time the deal closes. Parties to a deal must consider how to allocate the cost of uncertain events during that time period that can make a deal less attractive than expected. Which events will excuse a party from fulfilling its commitment?

In some deals, a *force majeure* clause provides that, in the event of an earthquake, flood, or other "act of God," a party will be excused from performing its contractual obligations. These provisions, of course, impose a cost on the counterparty. The fact that an "act of God" occurs does not mean it is God's will that a contract be terminated or one party's performance excused. Even if, say, an earthquake has rendered it impossible for a party to perform its end of the deal, this does not necessarily mean that party should be off the hook and the other party should bear the cost of its nonperformance. These events do make performance costly, perhaps prohibitively so, but nonperformance is costly as well. The parties need to decide how the cost of such an event will be allocated if the event occurs.

A related provision is a *material adverse change* (MAC) clause (or, as it is also called, a *material adverse effect* or a *material adverse event* clause). MAC clauses appear in merger and acquisition agreements and in debt agreements. Their function is to allocate the cost of external events that occur between the time a deal is signed and the time it closes. In the context of the sale of a company, for example, if a MAC clause is triggered, it allows the buyer to back out of the deal. But the trigger of a MAC clause is narrowly tailored. The typical trigger of a MAC clause begins with any "event" or "circumstance" that has or would reasonably be expected to have a "material adverse effect" on a company's "business, assets, properties, liabilities, operations, and condition." Judicial interpretation and additional terms, however, narrow the trigger substantially. First, the courts have defined a "material adverse effect" as a "sustained decline in business performance that is durationally significant and which would be material to a reasonable buyer."[13] Second, the MAC clause goes on to carve out of the trigger "changes in general economic conditions," "changes in conditions in the financial markets," "changes in the industry" in which the seller does business, "changes in regulatory, legislative, or political conditions," and many other varieties of change.

MAC clauses were invoked by many buyers who signed deals in late 2019 and early 2020 and then saw the economic implications of the COVID-19 pandemic play out. An issue in each case was whether the MAC clause excluded pandemics from its definition of a material adverse change. If it did, then the buyer would have to close the deal despite the pandemic. In November 2019, for example, LVMH agreed to acquire Tiffany & Co. for $135 per share in cash, or $16.3 billion in total value. When the pandemic hit, Tiffany was forced to close stores and furlough employees. LVMH would clearly not get what it had expected when it negotiated the deal. In September 2020, with the deal still not closed, LVMH declared that the deal was off, claiming that the pandemic was a MAC for Tiffany. The MAC clause that LVMH had negotiated with Tiffany carved out adverse effects associated with "any hurricane, tornado, flood, earthquake or other natural disaster," meaning that these events would not be considered MACs and therefore could not be a basis for LVMH's walking away from the deal. But because the agreement did not explicitly carve out pandemics, LVMH argued that the COVID-19 pandemic was a MAC and that LVMH could therefore walk. Litigation ensued, and the parties eventually recut the deal at a 2.6 percent lower price.[14]

3

BRIDGING VALUATION GAPS
WITH EARNOUTS

Imagine an acquisition of a biotech company that has a few drugs on the market generating revenues, plus a newly approved drug with potential to be highly profitable but facing some challenges to its commercial success. The seller will not accept less than $100 million for the ongoing revenue-generating business, and the buyer will not pay more than $150 million for that business. If this were the only business in play, the parties would have a straightforward negotiation over a price between $100 million to $150 million.

The new drug, however, complicates matters. It will have a major competitor that is already well established. To make matters even more dicey, it is not yet clear how insurers will handle reimbursement for the new drug. Nonetheless, the seller has done market studies and has had intensive discussions with insurers and believes that the drug will be highly successful. For simplicity, let's say the seller believes there is a 90 percent chance that the new product will add $100 million in value to the company, and a 10 percent chance that it will fail and add no value. The buyer has heard what the seller has to say about the drug's prospects and has read the seller's studies, but it has doubts about the seller's story. Again, for simplicity, let's say it believes the likelihood of a $100 million valuation to be 10 percent, and the likelihood of failure to be 90 percent. With these estimates, the seller will take no less than $190 million ($100 million for the established business plus the 90 percent chance of an additional $100 million) while the buyer will pay no more than $160 million ($150 million value for the established business plus the 10 percent chance of an additional $100 million). Is there any hope of a deal going forward? In the vocabulary of negotiation theory discussed in Chapter 1, is there a ZOPA? On the surface, it looks like the answer is no.

It is certainly not unusual for a buyer and seller to disagree on the value of a company. They may have different assumptions about how particular events will play out, or they may have different views on the organic growth of the company. The gap may be due to asymmetric information or symmetric uncertainty coupled with differences in judgment. If parties cannot reach agreement on a price, an *earnout* or *contingent value right* can potentially bridge the gap.

An *earnout* is a contractual arrangement under which an acquiror makes a supplemental payment to shareholders of an acquired company if the post-acquisition company's performance meets specified goals over a specified period of time. Because the acquiror must be able to locate the former owners of the acquired company to make such a payment, an earnout is practical only when the acquired company is either privately held or a subsidiary of a public company. A *contingent value right* (CVR) performs the same function as an earnout in the context of a public company acquisition. It entails issuing a security to the shareholders of the company being sold, rather than setting up a contractual obligation to them. The holder of a CVR is entitled to receive a payment if the company achieves specified performance objectives by a specified date. Some CVRs trade like a share of stock, and others must be held until maturity, at which point the post-merger company makes any payment that is due. The payment provided for by an earnout or CVR may depend on measures of post-acquisition financial performance, such as revenues or earnings, or it may depend on the occurrence of a specified event that will affect the value of the acquired company—for example, the development or launch of a product or a beneficial regulatory action, such as regulatory approval of a drug that is in development at the time the acquisition closes.[1]

At first glance, an earnout or CVR would seem to be a sensible pricing mechanism in cases where the value of a company being sold is uncertain—as is typically the case. After all, other sorts of transactions use pricing mechanisms that depend on measures of value that will materialize after a deal is made. As we noted in Chapter 2, for example, when technology is licensed, the licensee typically pays a fee based in full or in part on the revenues or unit sales it achieves after the licensing agreement is in place and the product is on the market. Commercial leases to retail stores are another example. Many include a base level of rent plus a percentage of sales from the store. And professional sports teams' contracts with athletes are chock-full of performance-based pay.

Especially when they are based on financial metrics, however, earnouts and CVRs can be difficult to design and implement. It is often hard for parties to agree upon a financial metric or combination of metrics that they expect will reflect the value of the post-acquisition company. Disagreement can also arise between buyer and seller over exactly what value should be measured. Is it the value of the company as a standalone entity? Is it the value of the company as an integrated part of the acquiring company? What if, after the acquisition, the buyer turns out to have priorities that conflict with maximizing the standalone value of the acquired company? These are fundamental issues on which a buyer and seller may be unable to agree. Thus, despite the inherent uncertainty and likely disagreement on valuation when a company is sold, earnouts and CVRs based on financial metrics are not as common as one might expect. Earnouts and CVRs based on external events are more common but only where there is an identifiable event to which value will be linked, such as regulatory approval of a drug.

Elements of an Earnout or CVR

The objective of an earnout or CVR is to adjust the total price paid for a company based on its performance following the acquisition. The parties must agree on a way of measuring the incremental value of the acquired company beyond what the buyer pays as a base price. The buyer pays that incremental value to the selling shareholders— or the CVR holders in the case of a public acquisition—at a specified date or dates after the acquired company has been operating under the acquiror's ownership.

Outside the life sciences sector, earnouts are typically based on financial metrics, such as post-acquisition revenues or earnings. Some formulae provide that the buyer will pay a simple multiple of a metric—for example, 20 percent of the target's average annual revenues measured over three years. Others use more complicated algebraic expressions incorporating multiple metrics. Earnouts may also incorporate nonquantitative milestones pinned to identifiable points in the post-merger integration process, such as the launch of a product or the closing of an anticipated deal with a major customer.

As a simple example, consider the earnout in Wipro, Ltd.'s acquisition of cMango.[2] The deal consisted of a $20 million upfront cash payment, to be followed by two potential earnout payments of $6 million at the close of each of the next two years. cMango's management would continue managing the company after the merger subject to a budget and business plan approved by Wipro, and with financial support from Wipro.

Wipro is an IT services company providing a broad range of services, including systems integration, information systems outsourcing, software development, and research and development services, to corporations globally. During the year of the acquisition, Wipro had revenues of approximately $3.5 billion and a workforce of approximately seventy-five thousand. cMango was a small, private, technology consulting firm that, prior to the acquisition, earned $13 million in annual revenues and had 120 employees working out of offices in the United States, United Kingdom, Singapore, and India. Much of cMango's consulting business focused on its clients' use of enterprise software products produced by BMC Software. Because this was the aspect of cMango's business that most interested Wipro, the earnout was specifically predicated on cMango's growing its revenues from that business. For the first year, Wipro would pay cMango's shareholders $6 million if BMC-related revenues reached at least $17 million. In the second year, another $6 million would be paid if those revenues reached at least $34 million. The earnout also provided for lower, graduated payments in the event that revenues fell short of those levels.

In the life sciences sector, earnouts take a different form. They are typically based on the achievement of milestones in the development of a new drug, medical device, or other innovation. Most of these milestones are nonfinancial, often marking key steps in a regulatory process, with payments triggered as the company passes each one. Assuming the innovation makes it to market, the attainment of a certain level of commercial sales might be another milestone. Earnouts based on nonfinancial milestones are less difficult to design than earnouts based on financial metrics. For that reason, mergers and acquisitions of life sciences companies are more likely to employ earnouts than deals in other sectors, as will be discussed below.

The Promise of an Earnout

Max Bazerman and James Gillespie describe several potential benefits of earnouts.[3] First, they characterize earnouts as a way to create value by exploiting differences in expectations between a buyer and seller. Take the example of the biotech company described at the beginning of this chapter. An earnout might bridge the gap in the parties' valuation of the new drug. The challenge will be for them to come up with a measure of value. But let's say they agree that if annual sales of the new drug reach $30 million within three years of closing, it is a reasonable bet, but not a certainty, that the drug will in fact add $100 million in value. With agreement on this measure of value, the parties might agree to a $125 million base payment at the time the deal closes, and an additional $80 million payment if annual sales reach $30 million within three years. From an ex ante perspective, the buyer would value the earnout payment at $8 million ($80 million times the 10 percent likelihood the buyer places on making the payment). Thus, according to the buyer's expectations, the cost of doing this deal would be $133 million in total ($125 million base price plus the $8 million)—a bargain, given its willingness to go as high as $160 million ($150 million for the existing business and $10 million for the new drug). The seller, meanwhile, would value the earnout at $72 million ($80 million times 90 percent) and the whole deal at $197 million ($125 million at closing plus the $72 million), which is greater than the $190 million it was willing to accept ($100 million for the existing business and $90 million for the new drug).

In a sense, the earnout creates an additional $64 million of value, in expected value terms; the seller viewed it as an expected payment of $72 million and the buyer viewed it as an expected cost of $8 million. That value creation is, of course, temporary based on predictions of the future. Eventually, the new drug will reach a $100 million valuation, or it won't, and the value of the company will be whatever it is. But the earnout gets the deal done. To say that the earnout can exploit a temporary difference in valuation is, in effect, another way of saying that it can bridge a valuation gap.

Bazerman and Gillespie also describe earnouts as powerful tools for revealing either side's true expectations. Albert Choi makes the same point in terms of a signaling model.[4] In the example above, if the seller truly has high confidence that the new drug will be successful, it can credibly signal that view (and the information on which it is based) by accepting a high earnout payment, and a low base price—lower than its valuation of the existing business. The signal is credible because, if the seller is wrong, it will find itself having sold the company at a price below its value. Likewise, if the buyer truly has little confidence that the drug will succeed, it should accept this same structure—a low base price and large earnout payment. If the buyer balks at a large earnout, that may indicate that it is more optimistic about the drug's success than it has let on—a valuable signal for the seller to note in negotiating a deal.

Earnouts can also be beneficial in situations of irreducible uncertainty where the parties value the company similarly but with a lot of uncertainty. In that situation, they share the risk surrounding the company's value. Consider a situation in which each party assigns a probability of, say, 50 percent to a certain event occurring in a target company's favor and creating $100 million in incremental value. If the event does not occur, the parties agree that the value of the company will be $200 million. The parties might therefore set an initial price of $200 million and agree to an earnout payment of, say, $50 million if the event does occur. They are taking the upside associated with this irreducibly uncertain future and sharing it fifty-fifty. In this setting, sellers often view an earnout as an "anti-embarrassment clause."[5] They avoid the scenario in which they sell for a low price, but then the good event occurs and they wind up embarrassed for having sold for too little. (Another term, more colorful, is "schmuck insurance.")

Finally, in deals where an acquired company's management team remains in charge of operations following its acquisition, an earnout creates added incentive to accomplish the work required to increase the value of the business. In the Wipro acquisition of cMango described above, cMango's primary shareholder continued to manage the company after the acquisition, so the earnout's strong incentive kept him focused on growing the company's business related to BSM Software. The earnout in this situation acted as incentive compensation.

LKQ Corporation's acquisition of EuroCarParts (ECP) illustrates all of these potential benefits of earnouts. In 2012, LKQ was the leader in aftermarket auto parts distribution in the United States, and was looking to make an acquisition in Europe to gain an entry point for that market. ECP, the market leader in the UK, was the natural candidate. Senior managers at LKQ approached Sukhpal Singh Ahluwalia, ECP's founder, CEO, and controlling shareholder, but there was a big valuation gap between the parties: LKQ offered roughly £200 million for the business, while Ahluwalia refused to sell for anything less than £300 million. LKQ would have preferred a straightforward cash deal, and indeed all of its prior acquisitions had involved simple cash payments at closing. But Ahluwalia was far more optimistic about the growth trajectory of ECP than LKQ was, and he wanted to get paid for the growth he expected. Not only did Ahluwalia know his company better than LKQ did, as is typical of most acquisitions, but Ahluwalia also knew the UK marketplace far better than did LKQ management. Ahluwalia's confidence notwithstanding, ECP's future growth was necessarily uncertain.

After lots of back and forth, the parties reached a deal at £280 million, payable at the closing, and an additional £55 million if ECP met certain earnings targets for 2012 and 2013. Importantly, after the closing, Ahluwalia would stay on as president of ECP, which would be a wholly-owned subsidiary of LKQ.[6]

The earnout served all of the purposes described above. It created value by bridging the valuation gap caused by the large difference in the parties' growth estimates. It reflected Ahluwalia's confidence in ECP's future growth. It meant that the parties would share the risk that the growth targets would not be achieved. And finally, the earnout gave Ahluwalia significant financial incentives to ensure that the growth targets were achieved.

And the result? ECP crushed its growth targets. Even before the earnout payment was due, it was so clear that the metrics would be met that LKQ paid Ahluwalia the full £55 million earnout. It was a steeper than expected price for the acquiror, but a payout that caused relatively little pain since, by hitting the growth targets, Ahluwalia had made several times that amount for LKQ's shareholders. Strategically, LKQ accomplished its objective of establishing a beachhead in the European marketplace. It went on to make a string of further successful acquisitions, and today, LKQ is by far Europe's largest distributor of aftermarket auto parts.

The Challenges of Financial Metrics in Earnouts

The description of earnouts above suggests that earnouts should be common. After all, asymmetric information and ex ante uncertainty are common in corporate acquisitions, especially when the seller is a private company. They are indeed common in acquisitions of life sciences companies, where they are based on a drug or medical device hitting regulatory milestones. But outside that sector, earnouts are typically based on financial metrics and are not so common. According to one report, outside the life sciences sector between 2019 and 2021, only 18 percent of acquisitions of private companies included earnouts.[7]

In this section, we will discuss earnouts based on financial metrics in acquisitions of private companies, and why they are less common than one might expect. Below we will address non-financial milestones in the context of CVRs used in public company acquisitions. This organization is solely for purposes of simplicity. In acquisitions of private companies, earnouts based on non-financial milestones are sometimes used, and in acquisitions of public companies, some CVRs are based on financial metrics.

Earnouts based on financial performance metrics are difficult to design and draft. First, it is often hard to specify a metric that reflects the value of the acquired company, especially if its operations will be integrated into the acquiring company's operations. Tracking the post-acquisition revenues attributable to the acquired company's products or services might be a reasonable metric. The value of the acquired business, however, could well depend in part on the extent to which the cost of generating sales or overhead costs will be reduced, in which case a formula based on revenues alone would be inaccurate. If the acquired company will be run as a stand-alone business, the profits would be a measure of value. But unless the business will be entirely separate from that of the acquiring company—with no shared functions or overhead—measuring profits would require the design of a tailored accounting approach, which could be a contractual nightmare. Profit-based earnouts are therefore rare.[8] Even if a measure of profits, revenues, or some other financial metric is identifiable and reasonably related to value, there is still the challenge of devising a formula that will translate that metric into a sufficiently accurate estimate of value— or, more specifically, incremental value above a base price paid at closing. What multiple, for example, should be applied to annual revenues or profits? This depends on predictions of long-term growth, which may differ substantially between the parties.

Second, the parties must set an appropriate length of time over which to measure post-acquisition performance. If the measurement period is short, the acquired business's true value might be obscured by a transient upturn or downturn due to events temporarily affecting the company, its industry, or the economy as a whole, or by transition issues related to the acquisition itself. A short earnout period might also be insufficient to measure growth. On the other hand, the longer the measurement period, the more likely it is that the business or business environment may have undergone so much change that the metric specified in the earnout will no longer fairly capture the value of the business.

A third reality complicating the search for financial performance metrics is that, after the buyer and the seller agree on the terms of an earnout and close their deal, they remain on opposite sides with respect to the outcome: the seller wants to receive more from the earnout, and the buyer wants to pay less. The party in control of the acquired company may be in a position to make operational or accounting decisions that affect the amount payable under the earnout. If the seller continues to run the business, as in the cases of cMango and ECP, it may be able to manipulate the company's operations or accounting to increase what it is paid without actually increasing value. It may even decrease the company's value in pursuit of a higher earnout. If the earnout is based on revenues, for example, a seller that remains in control of the company might spend too heavily on marketing, or offer a quantity discount that is not profitable.

If, instead, the buyer takes the helm, an earnout can encourage the opposite problem. To the acquiror, the earnout is, in effect, a very high "tax" on performance during the earnout period. With a profit-based earnout, for example, if the acquired business reaches its target during the earnout period, the acquiror has to make a payment to the company's former owners that will be many times greater than its profits. All other factors equal, therefore, the acquiror will have an incentive to keep profits low, perhaps by front-loading investments in new product development and organizational capacity-building, and delaying the reaping of financial gains until after the earnout period ends.

Fourth, if the acquiror controls the acquired company following an acquisition, it will want to maximize the value of its entire enterprise, which may not be consistent with maximizing the revenues or earnings, or even the standalone value, of the newly acquired firm. Other parts of the acquiror's enterprise may take on higher priority for resources, and the needs of the acquired company may have to be sacrificed. As a result, the performance of the acquired business may suffer, and payments under the earnout may reflect a value less than the standalone value of the acquired company, which is probably not what the seller intended.

As an example of this last challenge, consider the following earnout in PerkinElmer's acquisition of Sonoran Scanners, Inc. Sonoran was a small company that had developed a high-speed digital printing technology for the newspaper and graphic arts industries. Sonoran's machine was more expensive than competing technology, but it offered significant cost savings over the life of the product. This cost structure, coupled with Sonoran's small size, was a problem. If Sonoran went out of business, there might be no one available to service its machines, in which case customers would be unable to amortize the high upfront cost. Thus, Joseph Donahue, the founder and primary shareholder of Sonoran, sought a large acquiror that could assure customers it would be available for post-sale service.

PerkinElmer agreed to purchase Sonoran for an upfront payment of $3.5 million plus an earnout based on unit sales over the next five years. Under the terms of the earnout, PerkinElmer would pay Sonoran $750,000 if at least three machines were sold in the first year after the acquisition, $1.5 million (minus any first-year payment) if at least ten machines were sold by the end of the second year, and additional amounts if certain gross margin targets were met over the five-year payout period following the merger. Donahue would run the business under PerkinElmer's oversight and ultimate control.

Sonoran's business under PerkinElmer's ownership was a failure. PerkinElmer sold only one machine, so it paid nothing under the earnout. Donahue blamed PerkinElmer for the poor performance and sued the company, arguing that it had failed to promote Sonoran's product. Specifically, Donahue pointed to the fact that PerkinElmer had assigned a salesman to Sonoran's product who had no publishing industry experience and worked only part-time on this segment of PerkinElmer's business, and that it acted in bad faith by failing to invest enough in Sonoran's business to allow it to succeed. PerkinElmer had not, for example, offered discounted pricing on first units sold, as was customary in the industry, or otherwise spent appropriately on product promotion.

If PerkinElmer had done more to promote Sonoran's business, would it have performed better? Perhaps. But perhaps it had become clear, post-acquisition, that Sonoran's product was inherently uncompetitive with the alternatives to it in the market and could not ultimately be profitable. PerkinElmer may have determined that the cost of generating sales for Sonoran's product was not worth incurring, given the gross revenues it would likely yield. If that was the case, the earnout payment of zero accurately reflected the performance of the acquisition.

But there is another potential explanation. Perhaps, sometime after this deal closed, PerkinElmer made a strategic decision to emphasize other parts of its business. Even though Sonoran's product could have been sold profitably, PerkinElmer's management might have seen a chance for higher returns on its sales and marketing efforts elsewhere in the PerkinElmer enterprise. When a buyer is a large enterprise with many product lines, this kind of conflict between the buyer and a seller will often be present to some degree. From Donahue's perspective, a decision by PerkinElmer to sacrifice Sonoran sales for the sake of gains elsewhere in its business would violate the spirit of the earnout. But from the perspective of PerkinElmer's management, the fact that it had made an acquisition should not prevent it from taking actions in the best interests of the entire enterprise; any such constraint would be costly to PerkinElmer. This difference in perspective is quite reasonable.

Perhaps PerkinElmer and Sonoran should have addressed this point in their agreement, one way or the other. Whether purposefully or not, however, they did not address it. But as we will see, doing so is not as simple as it might sound.

Contractual Responses to Earnout Challenges

The prior section identified four challenges to designing an effective earnout. The first two are to develop an acceptable measure of value and to define the period over which that measure will operate. The ease with which parties can meet these challenges will be context-specific. The measure of value will depend on the business being acquired and the extent to which its performance over the few years following an acquisition can be translated into a reasonable measure of its value. The period over which the measure will operate is also context-specific. It will have to be long enough to register the performance it is intended to measure—for example, typical steady-state revenues or growth in revenues. Simply agreeing on a measure of value and a time period is often difficult.

The third challenge in designing an effective earnout is to limit the ability of the party in control of the company to manipulate the earnout to its favor, even if the measure of value is defined well and the time period is appropriate. If the buyer is in control of the company and the earnout is based on revenues, the seller will want to prevent the buyer from manipulating the company's operations and accounting to artificially reduce revenues during the earnout period. Conversely, if the seller is in control, the buyer will want to prevent the seller from artificially increasing revenues.

Writing an earnout that cannot be manipulated is difficult. To a large extent, earnouts are written in specific terms—as "rules" rather than broad "standards." The problem with rules, as we will discuss in Chapter 8, is that a party can sometimes avoid the impact of a contractual requirement by taking an action that violates the spirit of the deal but does not involve actual breach. A solution is to augment the rule with a standard reflecting the spirit of the earnout.

The terms of the earnout might, for example, include a provision that, while in control of the company during the earnout period, the seller will manage and account for sales in a manner *reasonably* consistent with past practice. This may make manipulation more difficult, but the use of this reasonability standard may nonetheless invite litigation. What is reasonable to one party might not be to the other, and it is difficult to predict how a judge, arbitrator, or jury would interpret the word. Furthermore, once the earnout is in effect, it can be difficult to distinguish manipulation from honest management of the company, especially if the business environment changes. This is a moral hazard problem we will discuss in Chapter 4.

Another approach is for the acquisition agreement to provide for some joint decision-making or oversight by the parties, rather than putting just one of them in complete control. Wipro and cMango took this approach. Their agreement provided that, while cMango's management would continue to run the business following its acquisition, it would have to submit a budget and business plan to Wipro's management for approval. This can work, but in some cases it might not: the parties could find themselves unable to agree on a decision that one regards as self-serving manipulation and the other claims is legitimate business practice.

It is the fourth challenge described above that is probably the most difficult to head off with contractual design. This is the possibility that, if the acquiror controls the acquired business during the earnout period, it will fail to maximize that business's performance because of post-acquisition changes in the overall strategic direction of the acquiror's entire enterprise. To prevent this threat to its earnout payment, the seller might reasonably insist that, during the earnout period, its business must be operated as though it were a standalone company. The acquiror, on the other hand, might insist on terms explicitly stating that it will be free to manage its enterprise as it deems appropriate. The parties might not be able to reach agreement even in principle.

Even if the seller and buyer can reach an agreement in principle, they may not find a way to put an agreement into contract language. What can be specified? The parties could agree that the acquired company will be managed reasonably consistently with past practice, but what if something different is needed for the acquired company to realize its potential value? Moreover, even if no significant break from past practice is needed, the parties could disagree on what *is* reasonably consistent. Similarly, an agreement can specify precisely what resources will be made available to the acquired company, but what if that prediction of needed resources is off-base, and the acquired business turns out to need more or different resources to meet its performance goal? These are not easy problems to solve by contract.

PerkinElmer and Sonoran had not included any contractual constraints on how PerkinElmer would manage Sonoran during the term of the earnout. Donahue sued nonetheless, claiming that PerkinElmer had not tried hard enough to sell his product. The trial court dealt with the silence in the contract in one way, and the court of appeals ruled in the opposite direction. The trial court stated that if Sonoran had wanted to constrain how PerkinElmer managed Sonoran during the earnout period, it should have negotiated contractual commitments. In the absence of those, the court declined to find them implicit in the earnout.[9] The court of appeals, however, ruled that, silence in the agreement notwithstanding, PerkinElmer had an implicit duty to make "reasonable efforts" to promote the Sonoran product. Since the trial court had not given Donahue an opportunity to prove that PerkinElmer failed to satisfy that duty, the court of appeals sent the case back to the trial court for trial on that issue. The trial court then found that PerkinElmer had met its obligation to make "reasonable efforts" to promote the Sonoran product.

One lesson from the PerkinElmer-Sonoran litigation is that, if an acquiror wants no obligations regarding how it will manage an acquired company during an earnout period, it should negotiate a term in the agreement explicitly stating it will have no obligations. Otherwise, a court might do what this court of appeals did, and find an implicit obligation where none explicitly exists. At the same time, however, sellers will probably not agree to an explicit statement that the acquiror has no obligation with respect to how the company is run during the earnout period. This would allow the acquiror not only to manage the acquired company as needed to suit the needs of its entire enterprise, but also to manipulate the earnout with impunity.

In contrast to the agreement between PerkinElmer and Sonoran, when AmerisourceBergen Corp. (ABC) acquired Bridge Medical in 2003, the parties agreed that, during the period of the earnout, ABC would be subject to sweeping commitments regarding how it would manage Bridge's business. This deal, too, resulted in litigation. ABC is a large distributor of pharmaceutical products. Bridge had developed barcode technology that helped to prevent errors in the provision of medications and other treatment to hospital patients. Having failed to turn a profit for several years, Bridge chose to find a buyer with greater capacity to sell the product. That search led to Bridge's sale to ABC.

Under the terms of the acquisition agreement, ABC paid Bridge shareholders an initial $27 million and committed to an earnout which, depending on whether certain earnings targets were reached over the subsequent two years, would add anywhere from zero to $55 million to that. The acquisition agreement further obligated ABC to invest in promoting Bridge's product, not to sell any competing product, and not to take any purposeful action to reduce the earnout paid:

> [ABC] agrees to . . . exclusively and actively promote [Bridge's] current line of products and services for point of care medication safety. [ABC] shall not . . . promote, market or acquire any products, services or companies

that compete either directly or indirectly with [Bridge's] current line of products and services.

[ABC] will act in good faith during the Earnout Period and will not undertake any actions during the Earnout Period any purpose of which is to impede the ability of the [Bridge] Stockholders to earn the Earnout Payments.[10]

As it turned out, sales of Bridge's products following the merger were weak and failed to generate the earnout payments that Bridge's selling shareholders thought they deserved. Bridge's former shareholders sued, arguing that ABC had breached the terms of the earnout by failing to put sufficient effort into marketing Bridge's product.

The court agreed with the Bridge shareholders. "ABC frequently breached its obligations under the merger agreement," it found. "Throughout the relationship, ABC promoted Bridge only where it was in [ABC's] interests to do so. Where it appeared that another partnership . . . would be more profitable, skullduggery and obfuscation became the order of the day. . . . Bridge became an occasional partner for scattered pieces of business, not the beneficiary of active and exclusive promotional efforts."[11] But the court also found that, even if ABC had fulfilled its obligations, Bridge's products would have failed in the market. Consequently, while it held ABC liable for breach of contract, it awarded no damages to Bridge's selling shareholders.

The ABC-Bridge earnout responded to both dangers sellers face when an acquiror controls the acquired company during an earnout period—manipulation of the earnout and sacrifice of the acquired company's business for the benefit of the acquiror's broader enterprise. But ABC's commitments appear to have gone too far. According to the court, Bridge's product was not a good fit for its market's needs and, if Bridge had been a standalone company, it would still have failed. In retrospect, it made no sense for ABC to commit efforts and resources to selling Bridge's products. The court was technically correct in ruling that ABC breached its agreement, because ABC's commitments did not depend on whether Bridge had a viable business. But the court was also correct that ABC owed Bridge shareholders no damages.

Like PerkinElmer, ABC won the case against it, but it lost in that it had to incur the heavy costs of litigation. How might it and Bridge have avoided all that expense? In principle, their agreement could have provided that, if Bridge's product proved uncompetitive in its market, ABC would have no obligation to actively promote it. But there could be a chicken-and-egg situation here. The competitive strength of a product depends in part on the resources devoted to marketing it. Writing a contract that imposed the right commitment on ABC might not have been so easy. And even if adequate contract language could be written, proving or disproving compliance with that commitment could be difficult—and expensive.

A earnout in a merger between QinetiQ and Cyveillance in 2009 raised the same issues—and also landed in litigation. Cyveillance was a small technology company headquartered in Virginia that specialized in cybersecurity. QinetiQ is a large defense contractor headquartered in the United Kingdom. With more than six thousand employees worldwide, QinetiQ provides a range of services to governmental defense ministries and departments, as well as corporate clients in the oil and gas, mining, transportation, and telecommunications industries.

A merger with QinetiQ would offer Cyveillance access to greater resources, including QinetiQ's salesforce, and it would offer QinetiQ a larger presence in the United States, which it viewed as an attractive market for its new and existing products. The parties agreed to a merger under which Cyveillance shareholders received $40 million upfront, and a revenue-based earnout under which they could receive another $4.5 million to $40 million.

During negotiations, Cyveillance proposed several provisions aimed at ensuring that its business would be fully supported and not at risk of being neglected due to other priorities QinetiQ might have. It sought commitments from QinetiQ, for example, that QinetiQ would act in good faith to maintain existing levels of business; preserve customer relationships; maintain adequate capital; make commercially reasonable efforts to recruit and retain employees; and continue bidding for new contracts as it had in the past. QinetiQ refused to commit to any of this, and instead agreed only that it would refrain from "taking any action to divert or defer revenue with the intent of reducing or limiting the Earnout Payment." This was a much more limited commitment not to manipulate the earnout, which left QinetiQ otherwise free to manage the QinetiQ-Cyveillance enterprise as it chose during the earnout period. Cyveillance accepted this narrow commitment.

After the merger closed, Cyveillance's management remained in place but QinetiQ assumed control of the company. At the end of the earnout period, Cyveillance narrowly failed to meet the minimum revenue target called for in the earnout, and Cyveillance shareholders did not receive any payment. One reason Cyveillance failed to meet the target was that QinetiQ prevented Cyveillance from entering into a potentially lucrative contract with a British intelligence agency.

Cyveillance shareholders sued QinetiQ for payment on the earnout, claiming that this action violated QinetiQ's commitment not to divert revenue. QinetiQ responded by explaining that its intent was not to reduce or limit the earnout payment. Rather, it said it had prevented Cyveillance from pursuing the contract because of US legal restrictions on certain agencies' abilities to work with vendors that have contracts with foreign governments. QinetiQ had feared that if Cyveillance entered into the contract with the British intelligence agency, QinetiQ might be barred from far larger contracts with US intelligence agencies in the future. QinetiQ thus acted to maximize the entire QinetiQ enterprise's opportunities rather than Cyveillance's near-term revenues. The court held that this motivation did not violate the terms of the earnout, and it supported its decision by pointing out that, in negotiating the earnout, QinetiQ had rejected a commitment that would have specifically covered this scenario.

These cases illustrate the obstacles that parties face when they try to bridge a valuation gap with an earnout based on a financial metric. Most fundamentally, a buyer and seller may not be able to find common ground on the question of whether the buyer should be permitted to take actions in the interest of its overall business that will imperil the achievement of the performance goals set for the acquired business. Even where there is agreement on this point in principle, the parties may not agree on how to draft terms that differentiate actions taken to promote the interests of the acquiror's overall enterprise from actions taken solely to reduce the earnout payment. And finally, even if terms can be drafted to their mutual satisfaction, a court may be unable to accurately determine whether the conduct of the party in control of the acquired business constitutes a breach of those terms. It may be difficult to distinguish an effort simply to minimize an earnout payment from an effort to promote the interests of the acquiror's broader enterprise. This last issue will be explored further in Chapter 4 on moral hazard.

An Attempt to Negotiate an Earnout

One often hears from experienced merger and acquisition bankers and lawyers that the idea of an earnout has come up in a negotiation only to be dropped along the way. We can provide an example of this happening in an earnout negotiation between two parties that we'll call Microvision and Installit, disguising their actual identities to preserve confidentiality. Installit had one primary product, which facilitated the installation of third-party software on laptop and desktop computers. It was a piece of technology that could be usefully integrated into Microvision's suite of software products.

Although both Microvision and Installit were highly motivated to make a deal, they could not agree on a price. Installit wanted $80 million, but Microvision put its value at $70 million. The parties compromised by entering into a nonbinding letter of intent at a price of $75 million plus earnout payments of $10, $15, and $20 million if specified revenue targets were met. Microvision would manage Installit following closing.

Microvision wrote the first draft of the merger agreement, which contained no restrictions on how it would manage Installit. Installit responded with the following:

> Purchaser hereby covenants and agrees . . . to (A) operate the [Installit] Business in good faith, in a commercially reasonable manner and in the ordinary course of business consistent with the past practices of Seller, (B) dedicate sufficient resources, including, but not limited to, working capital, marketing, and employee resources, to the operation of the Business, (C) refrain from taking any action which would result in the deferral of revenue otherwise than in the ordinary course of business, and (D) otherwise conduct the operation of the Business in accordance with the strategies, business methodologies and principles set forth in the Contingent Payment Schedule [which contained detail about how the company was managed prior to the contemplated acquisition].

A clever lawyer might find holes in this provision, but to a large extent, it would prevent Microvision from manipulating the earnout or sacrificing Installit revenues for broader Microvision interests.

Microvision responded with a revision of the proposed contract language—deleting the terms marked as strike-through and adding those in italics.

> Purchaser hereby covenants and agrees . . . to (A) operate the [Installit] Business in good faith, in a commercially reasonable manner and in the ordinary course of business ~~consistent with the past practices of Seller~~, (B) dedicate ~~sufficient~~ resources *to a reasonable extent as determined by Purchaser,* including, but not limited to, working capital, marketing, and employee resources, to the operation of the Business, (C) refrain from taking any action which would result in the deferral of revenue otherwise than in the ordinary course of business, and (D) otherwise conduct the operation of the Business in accordance with the strategies, business methodologies and principles ~~set forth in the Contingent Payment Schedule~~ *reasonably deemed prudent by Purchaser's senior management team.*

These changes restored nearly all discretion to Microvision in managing Installit. They did preserve Installit's protection against any shift of revenues by Microvision from the earnout period to the period after the earnout, which was certainly reasonable, and did subject Microvision to a standard of "good faith" and "commercial reasonability," which may have protected Installit's shareholders from provably abusive conduct (while also inviting litigation). But most of the protection that Installit wanted was gone.

Installit responded with the following, which essentially restored what Microvision had eliminated (inserting or reinserting what is in bold type and deleting the struck-through text):

> Purchaser hereby covenants and agrees . . . to (A) operate the Installit business in good faith, in a commercially

reasonable manner and in the ordinary course of business **consistent with the past practices of Seller subject to Purchaser's policies and procedures and reasonable oversight**, (B) dedicate ~~sufficient~~ resources, including, but not limited to, working capital, marketing, and employee resources, **consistent with Seller's current resources plus increased resources as reasonably necessary to support anticipated growth** ~~to a reasonable extent as determined by Purchaser,~~ to the operation of the Business, (C) refrain from taking any action which would result in the deferral of revenue otherwise than in the ordinary course of business, and (D) otherwise conduct the operation of the Business in accordance with the strategies, business methodologies and principles ~~set forth in the Contingent Payment Schedule~~ reasonably deemed prudent by Purchaser's senior management team.

The back and forth could have continued indefinitely without resolution. Rather than continuing that process, the parties ultimately scrapped the earnout and negotiated a single price.

Contingent Value Rights

As explained above, a contingent value right replicates the function of an earnout in the context of an acquisition of a public company. When a private company is acquired, its owners are often relatively few and identifiable, so they will be available to collect payments over the two or three years following the acquisition. An earnout is a straightforward contractual arrangement with them. When the company being acquired is publicly traded, however, the selling shareholders are numerous and not easily accessible after the merger. In this situation an earnout is not feasible, so instead, when the acquisition closes, the acquiror issues a CVR to the selling shareholders—along with the cash or shares that constitute the primary consideration. In some cases, a CVR takes the form of a security and trades on the NASDAQ or NYSE just like a share of stock, with its price changing as the market reevaluates the likelihood and size of its payout.[12] In other cases, a CVR is not tradeable, so the selling shareholders must hold it until it terminates, and then redeem it for the agreed payment (or not).

Like the earnouts discussed above, CVRs can be based on either financial performance measures or nonfinancial milestones. We've seen the challenges of tying payouts to financial metrics. CVRs (and earnouts) based on nonfinancial milestones are far less challenging—if such a milestone is identifiable for an acquired company's business. CVRs of this sort are most common in acquisitions of life sciences companies, where typical milestones are stages in the regulatory process of approving a drug or medical device.

Consider, for example, Forest Laboratories' 2014 acquisition of Furiex Pharmaceuticals, Inc. for $95 per share plus a CVR worth up to $30 per share. Forest Labs, founded in 1956, was a large, diversified pharmaceutical company. Furiex was a startup founded in 2010 whose high-profile drug in development, Eluxadoline, was attractive to potential acquirers.[13] At the time, Eluxadoline was in Phase III trials, the results of which would determine whether the Food and Drug Administration (FDA) would approve the drug for sale.

At the time of the acquisition, the future of Eluxadoline, and hence the value of Furiex, depended on both the FDA's approval and the assessment by the US Drug Enforcement Agency (DEA) of the potential for its abuse. The DEA categorizes all "controlled substances" into five schedules, or classifications, based on their addictive properties and potential for abuse, and it restricts their commercialization based on their classification. All other factors equal, a more restrictive classification means less commercial value. The most restrictive classification is Schedule I, which includes drugs such as heroin and LSD. Schedule I drugs have high potential for abuse and no accepted medical use. Sale of those drugs is therefore prohibited. At the next level, Schedule II drugs have a high potential for abuse, but they also have medical uses. Examples include oxycodone and morphine. Strict regulations apply to how Schedule II drugs are manufactured, used, handled, stored, and distributed. Schedule V drugs have the lowest potential for abuse and are subject to minimal restriction. This would be the best regulatory outcome for Eluxadoline.

To address the regulatory uncertainty, Forest Labs and Furiex agreed to a CVR with a payment contingent on both FDA approval and DEA classification. If the DEA determined that Eluxadoline did not have to be classified as a controlled substance at all, the CVR would pay out an additional $30. Short of that, it would pay out $20 for a Schedule V designation, $10 for a Schedule IV designation, or $0 for either a worse designation or failure to win FDA approval.[14] As it turned out, the FDA approved Eluxadoline and the DEA classified it as Schedule IV, which meant the CVR added $10 to the original $95 per-share price.

Conclusion

Earnouts and CVRs can be useful mechanisms for bridging valuation gaps between buyers and sellers—but not as useful as they may appear. In the life sciences sector, where they are based on regulatory milestones, they are common. In other deals, where value must generally be based on financial metrics such as revenues, they are frequently raised in negotiations but not commonly used. The core problems are, first, that it is difficult to draft, interpret, and enforce a financially-based earnout in a way that is accurate and that avoids manipulation; and second, that a buyer's interest in maximizing the value of its entire enterprise can conflict with a seller's interest in having an earnout reflect the value of its business alone.

4

MORAL HAZARD AND INCENTIVE DESIGN

When parties enter into a deal, they not only need to address the *ex ante* information challenges discussed in Chapter 3, they also need to anticipate *ex post* information issues. Will I be able to observe whether my counterparty is fulfilling its commitments? If necessary, will I be able to prove in court that it has breached our contract?

If a party is not able to observe and prove nonperformance, then it cannot rely on legal enforcement to ensure that it is compensated for the benefit it was promised but didn't get from a deal—and it may not be able to depend on the prospect of legal enforcement to induce performance of the deal. There may be good reason, nonetheless, to specify a commitment in a contract. Personal integrity, promotion of a good relationship, and maintaining a good reputation may be sufficient to motivate performance. But to rely on legal enforcement, a party must be able to prove to a court or arbitrator that a contract has been breached.

As an alternative to specifying a commitment in a contract and relying on legal enforcement of that commitment, parties may choose instead to create financial incentives that promote a desired outcome. Many deals rely partially or entirely on well-structured incentives, rather than commitments specified in a contract. Unfortunately, some deals get the incentives wrong, with regrettable results.

In this chapter, we explore the challenge presented when the actions taken to carry out a deal will be less than fully observable and verifiable to a judge—in economics terminology, deals in which *moral hazard* is present. In addition, we look at the design of incentives as a means of encouraging performance of a deal and avoiding unwanted conduct.

Moral Hazard: Unobservable and Unverifiable Action

In the deal context, *moral hazard* refers to a setting in which the self-interest of a party leads it to take actions that are contrary to the intent underlying the deal and possibly contrary to the explicit terms of the deal, and where the counterparty cannot fully observe those actions and cannot prove in court any violation of the contract. In the vocabulary of the moral hazard literature, the actions are *unobservable* and *unverifiable* in court.[1] Like adverse selection, discussed in Chapter 3, moral hazard is a problem of asymmetric information. But while adverse selection involves *pre-contractual* asymmetric information—Is the asset or service to be exchanged inherently good or bad?—moral hazard involves asymmetry in *post-contractual* information.[2] Is my counterparty performing as promised?

Like adverse selection, the concept of moral hazard was developed in the context of insurance—specifically nineteenth-century fire insurance. At that time, the term *moral hazard* covered what we now understand to be two distinct problems. First, it referred to a concern that insurance would attract people of immoral character—people who were dishonest or so careless that they would pose a greater risk to the insurer than would individuals of ordinary character. Such "moral hazards," to the extent they could be identified, would not be insured. That concern was later recognized as adverse selection. The second concern was that insurance would lead to a "temptation" to incur losses for which insurance would pay, even among people of good character—good people with insurance might act immorally.[3] In the 1960s, economists Kenneth Arrow and Mark Pauly, while recognizing that insurers face both challenges, differentiated between the two. Consistent with the economics framework, they described the "temptation" concern as a matter of incentives, and took morality out of the picture.[4]

The incentive problem an insurer faces is that, after it has agreed to insure a customer, that customer may be less careful in guarding against risks from which it is shielded, or it may overuse services that insurance covers. Once people buy health insurance, for example, they may overuse medical services. An insurer can write an insurance policy stating that only the costs of legitimately necessary medical services will be covered. This is an easy contract to *write*. But the insurer will often be unable to observe or verify whether a policyholder's claim meets this requirement. Was a course of physical therapy sessions medically necessary, or did the policyholder just see a chance to have the insurer pay for personal training and massage? To constrain such moral hazard, insurance companies incorporate into their policies such mechanisms as deductibles, copayments, and policy limits. When these mechanisms are written into insurance policies, they impose costs on policyholders, and reduce the incentive to consume unnecessary medical services.

Moral hazard is pervasive in economic relationships. In most employment relationships, for example, employees' efforts are not easily observed. As a result, some employees may not exert the degree of effort their employers expect. This is as true at the top of the corporate hierarchy as it is at the bottom. Not only is a CEO's effort difficult to observe, but CEOs are in a position to promote their own interests at the expense of their shareholders. For example, a CEO may want to preside over a large corporate empire—for reasons of personal prestige, higher pay, or better future job prospects.

Such a CEO could well have the power to pursue that objective by acquiring other firms or entering new markets, even if expansion conflicts with shareholders' interests. Shareholders may not be able to evaluate the merits of those decisions; the extent to which the CEO's actions are selfishly motivated may be unobservable. Even if shareholders suspect a CEO of undertaking an expansion for self-interested reasons, they may be unable to prove that in court—the motivations driving behavior are often unverifiable. Thus, if a CEO is determined to engage in self-aggrandizing empire-building, writing a contract that explicitly prohibits such conduct will probably not make a difference.

Moral hazard is also common, though often less obvious, in deals between companies. Consider a situation in which one party has licensed a technology that will be integrated into its product. If the licensee pays the licensor an upfront fee for the use of the technology, the transaction is uncomplicated: it is a sale of an asset, albeit an intangible one, for a single cash payment. But this is not how technology licenses typically work. More often, there is ex ante uncertainty or asymmetric information regarding the value of the technology, and the parties cannot agree on an upfront payment. Instead, they reach an agreement by which the licensor pays royalties based on sales of the product. The licensee pays for the technology as its value is manifested. But this response to an ex ante information challenge can create a moral hazard problem ex post. The ongoing burden of the royalty may create an incentive for the licensee to limit its use of the technology. If so, the licensor's expectations from the deal may be disappointed—especially if the license it granted was exclusive—and joint value may not be maximized.

Alliances between pharmaceutical and biotech companies often use this kind of royalty pricing structure. In those deals, the pharmaceutical company typically finances the biotech company's development of a drug, and in return for this investment, if the drug wins regulatory approval, the pharmaceutical company gains the exclusive right to commercialize the drug. The pharma company typically pays the biotech company a royalty equal to a percentage of revenues. Royalties of 12 to 15 percent of revenues are common.

The royalty is, in effect, a tax on the pharmaceutical company's revenues, and it may affect that company's conduct in a way that is disadvantageous to the biotech company. Without a contractual constraint, the pharmaceutical company will rationally make sales and marketing decisions based on revenues *net* of the royalty. Its negative response to the royalty tax can result in lower sales of the drug and therefore lower royalties to the biotech company. It might also lead it to favor another drug in its portfolio for which it pays no royalty, or a lower royalty.

Pharma company decisions based on net-of-royalty revenues would be inconsistent with both the expectations of the biotech company and maximization of joint wealth. To maximize joint wealth, the pharma company would devote resources to sales and marketing up to the point at which the marginal dollar spent equaled the marginal revenue generated, regardless of how the total revenues were distributed between it and the biotech company. Furthermore, the prospect of the pharma company failing to devote its full effort to selling the biotech company's drug could impair the latter's incentive to invest in the drug's development in the first place. Both parties have an interest in addressing the pharma company's counterproductive incentive by contract.

We saw this same issue in the context of earnouts in Chapter 3. Like a royalty, an earnout imposes a tax on the acquiror of the company—indeed, a much larger tax than a royalty—which the acquiror has an incentive to avoid to the extent it can. If an acquiror is operating under a revenue-based earnout, it has an incentive to push off recognition of revenues until after the end of an earnout period. Whether the acquirer would succeed in doing so would depend on whether such an action was observable and verifiable. Could the seller prove that the timing of revenue recognition was an intentional manipulation as opposed to a reasonable accounting practice?

The financing of the slate of movies discussed in Chapter 2, as an example of pre-contractual asymmetric information, also entailed moral hazard. Recall that, in that deal, a producer attracted outside financing for a slate of fifteen yet-to-be-selected movies. He formed a limited liability company (LLC) for the purpose of producing the movies, with the producer and some friends and family holding all the equity, and outside investors providing high-yield debt financing. The producer would control the selection and production of movies in the slate. The LLC was highly leveraged, which exposed the debt holders to moral hazard.

Moral hazard is inherent in any highly leveraged financing deal. Debt and equity have inherently conflicting interests. Equity gets an unlimited upside, while debt's upside is capped at its interest rate. Consequently, if equity holders control the company, they will tend to favor risky projects with high upside and downside. Equity will get nearly all the upside, and if the risk results in insolvency, debt bears a substantial portion of the downside. The more debt relative to equity in a company, the more downside risk the debtholders bear, and the greater the moral hazard associated with equity's control of the company.

In the context of the movie financing deal, the conflict was even worse. First, the parties' objectives might not have been aligned. The investors' interest was to maximize financial returns. The producer was presumably interested in a financial return as well, but he may have had a long-term interest in creating movies that receive critical acclaim, which may not translate into box office sales. In addition, if the producer were to produce other movies outside the slate, he might not put sufficient effort into the movies in the slate, or he might put the riskiest movies into the slate. If the investors were to lose their money, neither they nor a judge would have an easy time determining whether the slate's failure was the result of the producer's self-interested decisions or good faith judgments that did not work out. Hence, there was moral hazard in this deal, which as discussed below, the parties would have to address by contract.

Contractual Mitigation

To some degree, parties to business transactions may have to live with moral hazard. In the biotech-pharma alliance sketched above, there may be no other payment structure that would respond to pre-contractual asymmetric information with less moral hazard, and the deal might be attractive in other respects. In the movie financing deal, the producer must have substantial control over movie selection and filming. The producer is the producer, after all, and the investors are Wall Street finance types. They may have to accept some moral hazard.

But even if it cannot be entirely prevented, moral hazard can often be reduced. In the case of insurance policies, forcing policyholders to bear some of the cost of their actions—through deductibles, copayments, and other mechanisms—constrains moral hazard sufficiently to allow insurance markets to flourish. In a biotech-pharma alliance, if the royalty can be reduced, the pharmaceutical company's incentive to sell the drug will be improved. The typical structure of these deals, therefore, includes an upfront payment in addition to a revenue-based royalty. With an upfront payment, the royalty can be lower than what the biotech company would otherwise demand. And once the pharmaceutical company has made the upfront payment, that cost is sunk and will have no impact on the company's sales and marketing effort. Analogously, in the movie financing deal, reducing leverage by having the producer hold more equity relative to the investors' debt would reduce the incentive of the producer to promote his own interests at the investors' expense.

Another approach is to agree to contractual constraints, compliance with which will be observable and verifiable, that reduce the likelihood of conduct inconsistent with the objectives of the parties. In the movie financing deal, the parties relied on this approach to eliminate the possibility that the producer would allocate the worst movie opportunities to the slate and keep the best for some other arrangement. The solution was to require the producer to work exclusively on movies in the slate while the contract was in force. Because producing a movie outside the deal would be readily observable and verifiable, this source of moral hazard was eliminated. The financing agreement also placed restrictions on the types of movies the producer could include in the slate, specifying that they must be "live action 'genre films' (i.e. horror, action, thriller or adventure film)" intended for "wide domestic theatrical exhibition." In addition, each movie was subject to a specified minimum and maximum budget, and the individual budgets had to be disclosed to the investors. On all these points, any noncompliance could be easily observed and verified, and thus the contract terms reduced the possibility that the producer would produce movies with financial high risk or that sacrificed viewership for critical acclaim. These terms may not have eliminated moral hazard, but they kept it within sufficient bounds that the investors were willing to invest.

In a biotech-pharma alliance, the parties might agree that the pharmaceutical company will not sell a drug that employs the same "mechanism of action" as the licensed drug. This is an exclusivity commitment, but a limited one. It prevents the pharma company from marketing another drug that produces the same biochemical interaction with the same molecular target as the licensed drug. But the company can still market another drug that treats the same disease in a different way. Alternatively, in some deals, the pharma company agrees that, if it does sell another drug with the same mechanism of action, that drug will be included in the collaboration, with a royalty payable to the biotech company.

Yet another response to moral hazard is to increase the visibility of a party's actions. This, too, can be done by contract. Parties commonly agree, for example, to allow their counterparties to enter their premises to verify that they are fulfilling their commitments. They also agree to subject themselves to audits at their counterparty's request. The result is greater observability and verifiability. In biotech-pharma alliances, the parties create committees to oversee each stage of their work—for example, a drug development committee, a commercialization committee, an overall steering committee, and others. These committees, which have decision-making responsibility, typically have equal numbers of representatives from each company and thus must work by consensus. This requires a level of information sharing that allows committee members to proceed from the same base of information. An indirect function of these committees, therefore, is to provide visibility to each side into what the other party is doing and why.

Incentive Design

Another potentially useful response to moral hazard is to create financial incentives that align parties' interests. As discussed above, this is the rationale for deductibles and co-payments in insurance policies. Another example is the typical employment contract with a salesperson, which specifies that compensation will be based in part on his or her sales. A boss might not be able to observe how hard individual salespeople work or how well they interact with customers, but since the compensation scheme induces them to try to make sales, their actions may not need to be observed. It may be sufficient that the outcome of their work is observable. Similarly,

CEO compensation consists substantially of stock or stock options. The day-to-day details of how a top executive goes about leading a company will be largely unobservable and unverifiable, but stock-based pay may align the CEO's interests with those of shareholders in maximizing long-term share value. The design of incentive compensation, however, is not as simple as it may appear.

In some situations, incentives are deliberately designed to align interests, while in others, they are byproducts of payment arrangements that may or may not have been fully thought out. In alliances between pharma companies and biotech companies, the royalty that the pharma company pays to its biotech partner is not deliberately designed as an incentive; it is a form of payment agreed upon because the parties are too uncertain of the value of the drug to settle on a single, upfront payment. The fact that the pharma company keeps about 85 percent of the revenues from its sales efforts, however, provides it with an incentive to sell. And the fact that the biotech company gets about 15 percent of revenues provides it with an incentive to develop the drug in the first place. As we have discussed, the incentive created for the pharma company is not perfect, but it is not bad, and it can be improved with other contract terms.

Incentive Design in Response to Moral Hazard

The use of financial incentives to respond to moral hazard is inherently imperfect. Financial performance—whether of a salesperson, a CEO, or a pharmaceutical company—is a proxy for effort. Maximum effort is what an employer wants from an employee and what a biotech firm wants from its pharma partner, and it is all a counterparty can provide. But effort is difficult to measure. Financial outcomes, on the other hand, are relatively easy to measure. So long as financial outcomes are reasonably correlated with effort, reliance on financial incentives to respond to moral hazard can be the best alternative. But designing incentives is not simple. One need not look far to find counterproductive incentive arrangements.

The Tradeoff Between Risk and Incentive. There is a rich economics literature devoted to the design of incentive contracts. Beginning with the work of Bengt Holmstrom, economists have focused primarily on the principal-agent relationship.[5] An important strand of work analyzes the tradeoff between, on the one hand, providing incentives for desired performance and, on the other hand, allocating risk between principal and agent. To understand this tradeoff, consider the decision of a sales department manager in a company where salespeople are paid based on sales they bring in. To the extent that their success depends on factors beyond their control, such as the price and quality of the products they are selling and the price and quality of competing products, they face risk. They also face risk if measurement of their output is imperfect—for example, if they are not always properly credited for sales in which they played a role. Risk-averse salespeople will view such risks as costs, and will want higher compensation to make up for those costs. One way to reduce the cost is to shift some of the salespeople's compensation away from sales-based pay and toward a flat wage. Assuming the employer is risk-neutral (as is always the assumption in this literature), reallocating pay in this way imposes no cost in itself on the employer. But it will prove costly to the employer if the redesigned compensation scheme reduces the salespeople's incentive to work hard. In that case, the employer will, in principle, want to shift some of the cost back to its salespeople by reducing their total compensation. The salespeople and the manager, therefore, must negotiate a balance between risky incentive compensation and riskless base pay.[6]

Professional services firms, such as law firms and investment banks, also have to grapple with these tradeoffs in compensating their partners. Some firms take the approach of paying partners based on the business that they individually bring in—in the colorful language of business, this model is called "eat what you kill." This compensation system obviously encourages partners to drum up clients, but it creates irreducible risk for them individually, because winning new work with clients depends, to at least some extent, on factors outside a partner's control. At the opposite end of the spectrum is *lockstep compensation*, under which partner compensation is based solely on seniority within the firm. Lockstep compensation has the benefit of low risk, but adds nothing to the partners' incentives to bring in business.

Dysfunctional Incentives and Multi-Task Jobs. A second strand of the literature on incentives addresses *dysfunctional incentives*— those that push agents, acting in their own interests, to undermine the interests of their principal.[7] The theoretical, but quite realistic, situation giving rise to such dysfunction is a principal-agent relationship in which the agent is responsible for multiple tasks. Economists Bengt Holmstrom and Paul Milgrom, in their seminal article on the *multi-tasking model*, use the work of a schoolteacher as an example. A teacher is tasked with preparing students to score high on standardized tests and to attend to their intellectual development in other ways as well.[8] The upshot of the analysis is that, if paid based on student performance on standardized tests, teachers will devote their efforts to teaching to the test. More generally, an agent will perform the task for which the net gain is greatest—where the payoff to the work is high or effort is low.

In the law firm setting above, partners presented with an eat-what-you-kill compensation plan will focus on bringing in new business and devote less effort to serving the firm's existing clients, mentoring junior lawyers, or even developing good legal skills. For an incentive contract to induce an agent to exert optimal effort across a portfolio of tasks, the net gain for each task must be the same. Designing and implementing a compensation system that accomplishes that objective is generally not possible, especially for tasks whose performance is not objectively measurable.

Athletes' contracts provide more examples of this problem. Some Major League Baseball players get bonuses for hitting home runs. This may appear to make sense for both the players and the team owners; home runs often win games. But there are situations in which the right move for the team is for a batter to aim for a higher-percentage base hit to advance a runner. The job of a player is not just to swing for the fences all the time; a hitter has a multi-task job with different demands in different game situations. If, somehow, the player's contract could provide a bonus only for those home runs that should have been attempted given the game situation at the moment, then it would align incentives— but this is unrealistic.

Quarterback Ken O'Brien's 1987 contract with the New York Jets is one that continues to be cited for the dysfunctional incentive it created.[9] In the fall of 1986, O'Brien had led his team through a very strong start, racking up ten wins to one loss as the NFL's top-rated passer—but the Jets then went into an awful slide, with O'Brien throwing twelve interceptions in the last five games of the season. To turn the tide in the next season, the team and O'Brien signed a contract that included financial penalties for throwing interceptions. The clause had its intended effect in the sense that it did result in a much lower number of interceptions. O'Brien was highly focused on the objective for which he was rewarded (by not being penalized). Unfortunately, it also made O'Brien hesitate to throw the ball at some key moments when he should have. Throwing passes was the most important part of O'Brien's job and this new contract not only failed to reward him for doing so, it penalized him, in a probabilistic way, since an interception is a danger with any pass. The Jets thus created an unintended incentive for their quarterback to engage in game-losing behavior. For readers more familiar with soccer, imagine a contract by which a striker is penalized for every shot missed. The reasonable response would be to take fewer shots, which is not consistent with the striker's role in the team.

Back to American football, another player on the receiving end of a dysfunctional incentive was wide receiver Antonio Brown in his 2020–2021 season with the Tampa Bay Buccaneers. Brown's contract set his base salary at $1 million and provided for several bonuses he could earn on top of that, including a $250,000 bonus to be paid if he caught at least forty-five passes. As of the last game of the season, with just over two minutes left in the fourth quarter, Brown was still three catches short of that mark. But Tom Brady, the Buccaneers' quarterback who was well aware of Brown's bonus potential, was determined to make it happen. With the Buccaneers well in the lead and their spot in the championship playoffs secured, Brady used his last three downs to lob easy passes to Brown, and in effect also tossed him $250,000 of the Buccaneers' money, with no benefit accruing to the team's owners.

To be clear, these are not examples of moral hazard; they are examples of dysfunctional incentives. The origin of the problem is that the underlying action was unobservable and unverifiable—for example, whether the quarterback was throwing passes only at the right times (or the striker taking a shot on goal only when the risk of missing the shot was worth the upside of making it). So, the parties agreed instead to compensation based in part on outcomes—the number of interceptions (or missed shots). The problem in these examples is that the incentive structure induced dysfunctional conduct. In the end, deals that create dysfunctional incentives and deals that create moral hazard are similar in the damaging results they invite: both influence one party to the contract to take self-serving actions at the expense of the other.

Dysfunctional Incentives as Byproducts of Deals

In transactions between businesses, incentives are often byproducts of payment mechanisms, capital structures, or organizational arrangements designed for purposes other than incentive creation.

The "taxes" associated with earnouts and royalty payments are examples we have seen already. We describe two more below. First, in a venture-backed startup company, the granting of liquidation preferences to venture capitalists is typical, but can leave the founder and employees of the company unmotivated to exert optimal effort. And second, in a special purpose acquisition company (SPAC) the incentives of those in control are highly misaligned with the interests of shareholders.

Liquidation Rights in Startup Financing. In a typical venture capital (VC) financing of a startup, the VC takes convertible preferred shares, and the founder and employees take common shares. The preferred shares are convertible into common shares in the event that the startup goes public, so if an IPO is anticipated, the value of the two classes of shares rise or fall together, and all parties have an incentive to maximize the value of the company prior to the IPO. If, however, the company is more likely to be sold, a *liquidation preference* that the VC negotiates at the time of its investment can lead to a misalignment of interests and dysfunctional incentives.[10]

A liquidation preference gives the VC a right to a fixed amount of cash when the company is sold—but not if it goes public. Typically, but not always, the VC takes a "1x" liquidation preference, which means that, if the company is sold, the VC has a right to receive the amount that it invested in its preferred stock before the holders of common shares get anything. If the company is sold for an amount equal to or less than the VC's investment, the founder and employees get nothing. If the company is sold for more, the VC has the right to convert its preferred stock to common stock and share the proceeds of the sale pro rata with the founder and employees. At the time of a sale, the VC will calculate whether it can get more than its money back by converting its preferred shares to common stock. If so, the VC will convert and share the proceeds of the sale with the founder and employees, pro rata, according to the number of shares each owns. If not, the VC will take its liquidation preference, and the founder and employees will get the remaining proceeds of the sale.

This structure can create a conflict between the VC and the founder and employees. The founder and employees, who hold common stock, will get nothing from a sale at a price equal to or less than the VC's investment. So, if they see any prospect for the company to become more valuable, they will not want to sell at such a price. For the VC, however, if it sees a low likelihood of selling for more than its investment, it will want to sell, get its money back, and avoid the possibility of a loss later on. So, with respect to a sale at a price at or around the amount of the VC's investment, the VC and the founder and employees have conflicting interests. The VC typically has control of the company, either formally through board control or functionally through the power to withhold future financing. But a buyer of the startup may want the founder and employees to stick around, which they might refuse to do if they are going to get nothing out of the sale. Of course, this situation can set up a deal between the buyer, the VC, and the founder and employees, but that multiparty deal can be complicated, and there is no telling whether it will work out to the satisfaction of all. Perhaps more importantly, as the company approaches this point, if the founder and employees anticipate that the VC will try to sell, their incentive to create value will fade. In this situation, the liquidation preference is dysfunctional.

In some VC financings, the VC takes a 2x or 3x liquidation right, which amplifies its potential conflict with the founder and employees. Assume, for example, a startup backed by a single VC who invested $5 million and now owns five million preferred shares that are convertible into five million common shares. Assume further that the founders and employees collectively hold five million common shares. There are no other shareholders. If the startup is sold for an amount up to $15 million, the VC's 3x liquidation preference means that it gets *all* the proceeds. If the sale price falls between $15 million and $30 million, the VC gets $15 million, regardless of the sale price, and the common shareholders get the rest. If a sale price exceeds $30 million, the VC converts its preferred shares into common shares, because that allows it to do better than $15 million by taking its 50 percent pro rata share.

Under this arrangement, the founder and employees will oppose a sale below $15 million. Whereas that price yields a handsome return for the VC, it makes the founder and employees not a penny richer. If the buyer wants to retain the founder and some employees, it will have to negotiate a deal, at some cost and with an uncertain outcome. The same might be true if the sale price exceeds $15 million but not by much. For the founder and employees, the idea of selling becomes increasingly attractive as the price rises higher above $15 million—but the VC has no additional incentive to sell the company at a price above $15 million, unless it can sell for over $30 million. Thus a sale between $15 million and $30 million could also be contentious. The founder and employees may push for a higher price, while the VC may want to take the bird in the hand. Furthermore, earlier in the company's life, if the founders and employees do not foresee a sale much above $15 million, they might not bother trying to grow the company at all. VCs' liquidation preferences thus create dysfunctional incentives and potentially lost value.

SPACs. Even worse are the dysfunctional incentives inherent in the structure of special purpose acquisition companies, or "SPACS," an investment vehicle that became a financial fad beginning around 2019.[11] SPACs are pitched as a deal through which public investors can invest in a private company as it goes public. The process begins with a SPAC going public in an IPO—by convention, selling "units" consisting of one share and a warrant for $10 per unit. The

SPAC then has a limited time—typically, eighteen or twenty-four months—to identify a private company with which to merge (or "de-SPAC") and thereby bring that company public and invest the cash it collected in its IPO. If the SPAC does not merge within the specified period of time, it is required to liquidate and return the money its public shareholders invested. If the SPAC succeeds in negotiating a merger, it proposes the deal to is public shareholders, at which point they have a right to redeem their shares rather than participate in the merger.

A SPAC is controlled by a "sponsor," a limited liability company sometimes backed by a private equity fund and other times backed by an individual or individuals with no other affiliation. The sponsor appoints the SPAC's directors and management, who typically are individuals who control or are affiliated with the sponsor. The sponsor takes twenty percent of the SPAC's post-IPO shares at a nominal price, and distributes some of those shares to the SPAC's directors and management. The sponsor also makes an investment of several million dollars, which the SPAC uses to pay its IPO expenses and other expenses it incurs between the time of the IPO and a merger or liquidation.

The sponsor, directors, and management have one job: to find a private company with which to negotiate a de-SPAC merger. Although they have a fiduciary duty to act in the interests of the SPAC's public shareholders, their incentives in the search for a target and the negotiation of a merger are not aligned with the shareholders' interests. The source of the conflict lies in the fact that they and the public shareholders have different classes of shares with rights that differ in important respects. A key difference is that, if a SPAC fails to merge and therefore liquidates, the public shareholders get back the cash they invested in the SPAC's IPO, but the sponsor, directors, and management get nothing. Moreover, the sponsor loses its initial investment of several million dollars. A failure to merge is thus a disaster for the sponsor, the directors, and management.

On the other hand, if the SPAC merges, the sponsor stands to make tens of millions of dollars, and the directors and officers stand to make hundreds of thousands on the shares the sponsor transferred to them (and on any ownership interest they have in the sponsor). Consequently, the sponsor, directors, and officers have a strong incentive to avoid liquidation. They will prefer *any* merger over liquidation.

To make matters worse, the structure of a SPAC makes it highly unlikely that it will strike a deal with a merger partner that is worth the $10 per share redemption price available to public shareholders.[12] The SPAC structure is highly dilutive of shareholder equity. On average, research has shown that once one takes into account dilution and the dissipation of cash in merger-related banker fees, SPACs on average have only about $5 or $6 in net cash per share at the time they merge. It stands to reason, and it has been borne out statistically, that target companies treat SPAC shares as being worth the amount of their underlying cash when they negotiate how much of their company to exchange for SPAC shares.[13] So the economics of a SPAC, coupled with the incentives of the sponsor, directors, and officers create a deck severely stacked against SPAC shareholders.

In light of this, one might expect essentially all SPAC shareholders to exercise their redemption right rather than go along with a proposed merger. But just as the sponsor, directors, and management have an incentive to enter into a bad merger rather than liquidate, they also have an incentive to minimize redemptions. Many merger agreements contain minimum redemption requirements for a merger to close. Consistent with these incentives, SPAC sponsors, directors, and managers are often less than forthcoming with information they disclose to shareholders in connection with a de-SPAC merger. Most fundamentally, they routinely fail to disclose to shareholders how little cash there is underlying their shares and therefore how little they can expect to get from a proposed merger. These disclosure failures are now the subject of litigation brought by shareholders, which so far has gone the shareholders' way.[14] By late 2021, after SPAC shareholders had suffered severe losses in the vast majority of post-de-SPAC companies, redemptions finally approached 100 percent and the SPAC debacle started to fade away.

GigCapital3, a SPAC that went public on May 18, 2020, provides an example of SPACs' dysfunctional incentives at work. Gig3's founder, Avi Katz, followed the SPAC playbook, forming an LLC to serve as sponsor, issuing about five million "founder shares" to the sponsor essentially for free, and investing $6.5 million for another 650,000 shares. Katz appointed himself CEO and close associates as directors. All were given founder shares or interests in the sponsor. Hence, all would gain from a merger, and lose from a liquidation. Gig3's public shareholders, on the other hand, would benefit only from a merger that would yield more value than the $10 per share they would receive if they redeemed their shares.

On May 6, 2021, GigCapital3 merged with Lightning eMotors, an electric vehicle company. For public shareholders, the merger was a disaster. Six months after closing, the company's share price was down 40 percent, which is about where the price stood a year after the merger. As this book went to press, the share price was down about 99 percent. If the insiders still held their shares at that point, it was not a happy ending for them, either. But to the extent they sold shares in the first year or so, they did very well. If the sponsor sold its shares for $6, for example, it received over $30 million—a roughly fivefold gain on its $6.5 million investment.

Although the depths to which Lightning eMotors' share price fell might not have been predictable, the fact that this would be a bad deal for Gig3 public shareholders was predictable. Taking into account the dilution and dissipation of Gig3 shares, there was less than $5 in net cash underlying the shares that Gig3 contributed to the merger. It stood to reason that Gig3 shareholders would receive about the same value from Lightning eMotors shareholders in return. It was predictable, therefore, that Gig3 shareholders who chose not to redeem would have shares worth about $5 after closing.

So, why didn't all Gig3 shareholders redeem their shares? The answer may lie in the fact that Gig3 did not adequately disclose to shareholders how little net cash they would be investing in the merged company. A class-action lawsuit has been filed on behalf of the shareholders who did not redeem their shares.[15] While Gig3 was extreme in the amount of cash it drained from public shareholders, it was not unusual in its failure to disclose clearly how much cash was left.

5

ASSET SPECIFICITY AND LONG-TERM CONTRACTS

In some situations, for an exchange to take place between two parties, one or both must make an *asset-specific investment* (or, equivalently, a *relationship-specific investment*). This is an investment whose value is dependent on the cooperation of another party; it would have a substantially lower value, and perhaps no value, outside the relationship with that party.[1] A classic example is an oil well in an area served by a single means of transporting oil to a refinery, such as a pipeline. Without the cooperation of the pipeline owner, the oil well will be worthless. The value of the well is "specific" to the pipeline. Hence, the well will be drilled only if the owner of the right to the oil has a long-term agreement with the pipeline owner to transport oil from the well.[2] In this chapter we will explore deals involving such investments and the contractual responses parties make to protect their interests.

Even when there is no such upfront investment required, it can also make sense for parties to enter into a long-term contract if they want to develop a business relationship that they expect will be valuable over time. Where this is the case, it often is not feasible to specify detailed commitments by contract, but the parties can set out key terms while leaving room for flexibility regarding how their venture will develop. For example, if they hope to develop a technology together, or to build a business together, they can specify basic terms and leave the rest to evolve. One can conceptualize this as a relationship-specific investment, with the long-term contract providing broad outlines.[3]

Asset-Specific Investment and Opportunism

The economist Oliver Williamson initially developed the concept of *asset specificity*, which he defined as "the degree to which an asset can be redeployed to alternative uses by alternative users without sacrifice of productive value."[4] The oil well noted above, for example, has a high degree of asset specificity because it cannot be redeployed, and while perhaps another mode of transportation could be arranged, that would entail much greater cost. The degree of asset specificity of the investment in the well can be measured by the difference in transportation cost between the already-present pipeline and the next-best alternative. Asset specificity is thus a matter of degree. Nonetheless, it is often convenient to analyze business relationships in terms of whether they do or do not involve asset-specific investments. We will adopt that convention here.

In the vocabulary of the economics literature, the danger inherent in an asset-specific investment is that, absent protection, the party on which the investment depends may "hold up" the party that has made the investment—that is, it may act "opportunistically" after the investment has been made to exploit the dependence of the latter. To return to our oilfield example, if the well owner has already drilled the well and has no alternative means of transporting oil from its well, the pipeline owner might decline to transport the oil unless the well owner pays a high price—potentially a price that extracts nearly all the well owner's profit.[5] If there were an alternative, but more costly, means of transportation available to the well owner, the pipeline owner could demand a price equal to the cost differential minus a penny. Unless the possibility of holdup is addressed in advance, an asset-specific investment will never be made—the well will not be drilled.[6]

Asset-specific investments may also be made over the course of a long-term business relationship, as opposed to at the start. Consider a deal between a baseball team and a regional sports television network—say, the New York Yankees and the Yankee Entertainment and Sports Network (YES), a majority of which is owned by media companies and outside investors. The network commits to broadcasting games locally and the team commits to do what it always does: play baseball. The team makes no asset-specific investment and, at the outset, neither does the network. But over the course of the relationship, the network will invest in marketing and advertising its broadcasts of the team's games, and in doing so make asset-specific investments that can pay off only if the network continues to broadcast those games. It serves the interests of both parties that the network make these investments. The team, therefore, enters into a long-term contract with the network under which the network will continue broadcasting the team's games. We will return to this deal in Chapter 7.

Asset specificity can also be bilateral, where each party's investment is dependent on the other party. In that case, opportunism may not be a problem, or at least not as large a problem as with one-sided asset specificity. One party's threat not to deal with the other would not be credible, since that party, lacking good alternatives, would suffer too. The balance of dependence between two parties can change over time, however, so the fear of holdup could still deter one or both from investing if the holdup possibilities are not addressed in advance.

There are two potential responses to a business situation in which asset-specific investment is needed. One response is integration—for one of the two companies to acquire the other. If a buyer and seller integrate, the danger that one will hold up the other is eliminated. But there could be a cost to integration. The incentives of the managers of one or the other parties will be diminished since the two businesses now share profits and work within a larger enterprise, potentially with an attenuated incentive compensation structure. The second response is for the parties to enter into a long-term contract that provides assurance to the party making the asset-specific investment that the relationship will continue long enough to justify the investment.[7] Economists Oliver Hart, Sanford Grossman, and John Moore developed a "property rights" theory of the firm, which elucidates the choice between integrating and relying on a long-term contract. We will discuss only the long-term contract option.

Long-Term Contracts as a Response to Asset-Specific Investment

The objective of a long-term contract in the context of an asset-specific investment is to ensure that the party that makes the investment will have a reasonable likelihood of amortizing that investment. If, for example, a company is considering building a customized manufacturing facility to serve a particular buyer, the company will seek from the buyer a commitment to continue buying for a long enough period of time to justify the investment in the facility. Similarly, if the company's manufacturing facility will depend on the availability of a unique input from a particular supplier, the company will seek a commitment from the supplier to supply the input for a sufficient period of time. In the oilfield example, the would-be well owner would get a commitment from the pipeline owner for a period that matches the expected productive life of the well.

Empirical research has confirmed the use of long-term contractual commitments to support asset-specific investments.[8] For example, Paul Joskow has shown that power generators generally enter into long-term contracts with coal mines when they will be reliant on a mine's output. In situations where a power generator is located next to a mine—and hence is probably dependent on that mine—he finds a strong tendency for the mine and the generator to be bound by a long-term contract. Joskow also finds that long-term contracts are used where power plants are designed to use a type of coal that is costly to access in a given region, and where power plants buy large quantities of coal from single mines.[9] In the latter situations, Joskow inferred that plants would have difficulty making large purchases at similar cost from alternative sources, and that the investments made to build the plants were likely asset-specific.

In another study, Victor Goldberg and John Erickson analyze oil refineries' contracts for the disposal of petroleum coke.[10] Petroleum coke is a byproduct of a "coking" process that extracts light and medium fuels from the heavy oils left over after crude oil is distilled. By coking the heavy oils, a refinery converts low-value residual oil into higher-value fuels. The refinery, however, must dispose of the petroleum coke before too much builds up in its "pond," and transporting coke is expensive. Many refineries, therefore, do not invest in coker units; instead, they use the heavy oils to produce lower-value products. Refineries that do invest in cokers sell the coke to companies that "calcine" the coke—meaning they extract carbon from it. The calcined coke is an input in the production of carbon anodes used to produce aluminum. Goldberg and Erickson studied two primary choices that refineries had for selling coke to a calciner. One was to sell the coke to Great Lakes Carbon Corporation (GLC), owner of several calciners with substantial storage capacity in locations close to refineries, and which supplied calcined coke to multiple aluminum companies. The other option was to sell the petroleum coke to a single aluminum company that calcined the coke for its own use in producing carbon anodes. For the moment, we will set aside the latter scenario (but will return to it in Chapter 6, where we discuss quantity adjustment in long-term contracts). Let's consider here an instance where a refinery sold coke to GLC, the intermediary calciner.

Both coking and calcining require major investments in capital equipment. Furthermore, because petroleum coke is expensive to store and transport, a refinery would not invest in a coker unless it had a long-term contract under which it would sell calcined coke. The various calciners owned by GLC each had several long-term contracts with refineries, which they had entered into at the time the refineries built their cokers. So, in the context of this exchange, the refineries' investments in cokers were asset-specific, but GLC's investments in its calciners were not: GLC had several refineries from which it could source coke, and did not have to worry about being held up by any one of them. GLC's large storage facilities, meanwhile, also protected it from disruptions in the demand for its product. It could withstand slowdowns in the aluminum markets when its customers paused their purchases of calcined coke and inventories built up. GLC's contracts with refineries provided that GLC would take any and all coke the refineries produced, which fully protected the refineries' investments in cokers.

A party making an asset-specific investment may not be able to obtain full protection from a counterparty in the form of guaranteed purchases, for example. But there are other mechanisms that can provide substantial protection. One is for the counterparty to agree to an exclusive relationship. Exclusivity converts a situation of unilateral dependence into one of bilateral dependence. The party making the asset-specific investment is dependent on its counterparty by the very nature of its investment, but with an exclusive contract the counterparty is also dependent, because it is contractually prevented from seeking an alternative deal. The counterparty, therefore, is poorly positioned to act opportunistically. Exclusivity alone, however, may not fully protect an asset-specific investment, since the quantity the counterparty may need to buy or sell over time may turn out not to be sufficient to amortize the asset-specific investment.

A counterparty might also push back against exclusivity. Consider a deal between two companies that, to preserve confidentiality, we will call SemiCo and TestCo. SemiCo is a large manufacturer of semiconductors, and TestCo is a startup with a new technology for testing advanced semiconductors. Testers are critical to the semiconductor manufacturing process, and are customized for particular semiconductors. Each semiconductor produced must be tested with its own individual tester. Especially at the high end, semiconductors and testers are designed in parallel.

SemiCo was developing a new line of high-end semiconductors for which it believed TestCo's new testing technology would be particularly well suited. To meet SemiCo's expected demand for testers, TestCo would have to construct a manufacturing plant specifically for SemiCo's new semiconductors. To protect TestCo's asset-specific investment in the plant and equipment, the two sides entered into a long-term contract. We will revisit this deal in Chapter 6, where we will discuss the ways in which the parties agreed to adjust the quantity of testers that SemiCo would purchase as it saw the market's response to its new semiconductors, but for now suffice it to say that TestCo received sufficient assurance to support the asset-specific investment in the plant and equipment.

One element of the deal was *quasi-exclusivity*—an arrangement short of full exclusivity. SemiCo would purchase from TestCo all the testers it needed for this new line of semiconductors, subject to a *second source* arrangement. SemiCo would have the right to purchase 15 percent of its testers from a third party that would produce TestCo testers under a license from TestCo. In addition, if TestCo failed to meet its obligations to supply testers, SemiCo could purchase all testers from the second source. The reason behind this arrangement was that SemiCo refused to expose its new line of semiconductors to the risks that would come with a completely exclusive supply contract with TestCo.

Long-term contracts adopted to support asset-specific investments must do more, however, than prevent opportunistic behavior. They must regulate the relationship between the parties over a period of time in which some aspects of the business environment, and possibly the parties themselves, will likely change. A complete state-contingent contract is rarely feasible, and a party making an asset-specific investment will always bear some risk that circumstances will change in a way the contract does not address. Chapter 6 will address ways in which long-term contracts can provide for adjustment to changed circumstances while still providing the assurance needed. And in Chapter 7, we will address the most extreme way of responding to change: exiting the relationship without destroying value.

Long-Term Contracts in the Absence of Asset-Specific Investment

Protection of an asset-specific investment is not the only function of a long-term contract. Long-term contracts are often present when no such investment is apparent. So, these contracts must create some other value. Otherwise, the parties could conduct their business with no contract or with a series of short-term contracts. Economists Oliver Hart and John Moore have identified another theoretical function of long-term contracts. They observe that, in a long-term business relationship, where there is uncertainty regarding the parties' future needs, cooperation and flexibility are valuable. Very often, parties will not be able to fully specify in advance what they expect of one another under varying circumstances. In Hart and Moore's theoretical model, a long-term contract that specifies key elements of a deal can facilitate flexibility and cooperation with respect to other important but unidentifiable aspects of the parties' future relationship. Hart and Moore posit that a party's compliance with the key terms specified in the long-term contract—which they refer to as "reference points"—will go a long way toward engendering cooperation more broadly. One can conceptualize the cooperation that Hart and Moore envision as a self-perpetuating sequence of parties investing in their relationship and reaping the rewards from that investment. It is thus not entirely different from asset-specific—or, perhaps more precisely, relationship-specific—investment in more tangible assets that create value for the parties.

Hart and Moore's theory comports with intuition and casual observation. In the long-term deal referred to above between a baseball team and a regional television network, one can imagine the extent to which the two parties would need to develop a cooperative relationship with respect to numerous situations that they cannot adequately address in a contract. When should the team make players available for on-air interviews? Which players? To what extent should the team and the network put on promotional events, and who should participate? The list could go on. So long as each party complies with the key terms included in the contract, it is reasonable to expect broader cooperation to develop and for each party to benefit from such cooperation. On the other hand, if one party breaches a key term, one might expect cooperation to break down.

Asset-Specific Investment and Cooperation in the Absence of a Long-Term Contract

Whereas Hart and Moore posit that long-term cooperation can be engendered through a very incomplete long-term contract, other theorists have shown that a contract is not necessarily required at all. Economists Benjamin Klein and Keith Leffler provided a model showing that, when it is not possible to specify product quality by contract, a seller with repeated interactions with a buyer will nonetheless deliver a product that meets the buyer's needs (not too surprisingly).[11] Legal scholar Stuart Macauley made the same point much earlier through his research showing that many business relationships are conducted with no reliance on legal enforcement.[12] In these settings, the value of future business is greater than the value that can be achieved by holding up one's counterparty or declining to cooperate. In the words of Benjamin Klein, Robert Crawford, and Armen Alchian, a mutually valuable relationship can endure based solely on an "implicit contractual guarantee enforced by the market mechanism of withdrawing future business if opportunistic behavior occurs."[13]

But to say that a formal long-term contract is not always necessary to protect an asset-specific investment or to promote cooperation is not to say it is always possible to forego one. The contracts described in this chapter were essential in providing the assurance needed to justify the asset-specific investments that were made and the cooperation that developed.

6

QUANTITY AND PRICE ADJUSTMENT
IN LONG-TERM CONTRACTS

As we saw in Chapter 5, a long-term contract is a means of providing the assurance needed for a party to make an asset-specific investment. And even without asset-specific investment, a long-term contract can be useful in promoting a mutually valuable working relationship in which cooperation is engendered. To accomplish these objectives, a long-term contract locks in elements of a deal. Yet the parties to a long-term contract often know that market and other conditions surrounding their exchange will not be static, and may want certain elements of their deal *not* to be locked in. Two elements of a deal that may require adjustment are the parties' commitments regarding what *quantity* of goods or services will be sold over the contract period and at what *price*. Failing to allow for such adjustments in response to changes in the business environment can lead to value-destroying conduct as cooperation ceases and one party or the other seeks to get out of the deal. In this chapter, we look at quantity and price adjustments in the context of several deals.

Quantity Adjustment

When parties to a long-term supply contract expect changes in market supply or demand for a product, they will likely want to provide for flexibility in the quantity of goods sold under the contract.

Whether a deal allows for more or less flexibility will reflect the extent to which each party depends on the other. If a supplier has made an asset-specific investment, it will want some assurance that it will earn a return on that investment. Similarly, if the buyer makes an asset-specific investment, it is banking on the delivery of a certain volume of goods. The extent to which a counterparty can provide assurance and thereby protect its counterparty's investment depends on the expected fluctuation in the counterparty's business over the course of the contract. In some cases, a counterparty will provide all the assurance needed, and in other cases it will provide something less, and the parties will share the risk inherent in the deal. An asset-specific investment may still be worth making even if the party making it does not get complete protection under all circumstances.

A long-term supply contract may provide for delivery of a specified quantity of goods at designated times over the term of the contract. Such a *fixed-quantity* contract makes sense only if the supplier has reasonable certainty regarding its ability to produce that quantity over time, and the buyer has reasonable certainty that it will need that quantity. Alternatively, a *requirements* contract provides that a supplier will provide whatever quantity of goods the purchaser needs, which can change over the term of the contract. Conversely, an *output* contract provides that the supplier will deliver the entire output of a specified plant or plants, which may vary over the term of the contract. If a buyer is dependent on the seller and expects to face fluctuating demand for its final product, a requirements contract can be joint-value maximizing— as long as the seller can replace lost sales when the buyer's requirements are low. Likewise, if a seller is dependent on a buyer, and the seller is not sure that it can deliver a precisely specified quantity, an output contract can be jointly attractive—as long as the buyer has alternative sources of supply.

As an example of how these different types of contract make sense with different counterparties, we revisit the long-term deals described in Chapter 5 between oil refineries that produce petroleum coke and parties that operate calciners—the subject of research by economists Victor Goldberg and John Erickson.[1] Recall that petroleum coke is a by product of a coking process that converts low-value residual oil into higher-value fuels, and that calciners extract carbon from petroleum coke to produce carbon anodes needed by aluminum producers.

The contracts between refineries and Great Lakes Carbon Corporation obliged the latter to take any and all coke that the refineries produced. Because GLC purchased coke from many refineries, had large storage facilities, and had many customers for the coke it produced, it could agree to *output* contracts with the refineries—contracts under which the refineries could unload as much or as little coke as they produced. These contracts with GLC gave the refineries maximal assurance that they would not be stuck with unwanted coke, and hence allowed them to invest in cokers with confidence.

Goldberg and Erickson also analyzed deals where, instead of selling to an intermediary like GLC, a refinery sold its coke directly to an aluminum producer that had its own calciner and produced its own carbon anodes. Those contracts were different from the GLC contracts. Unlike GLC, an individual aluminum company could not commit to taking whatever quantity of petroleum coke a refinery produced. It had limited capacity to store coke, and its need for carbon anodes would fluctuate with upturns and downturns in demand for its aluminum. These contracts, therefore, were written to balance the refinery's need to unload coke and the aluminum company's limited ability to store coke until it was needed. The contracts generally gave the aluminum company some control over the quantity of coke it would take, while specifying a required minimum purchase in a given time period. Some contracts also allowed the aluminum company to avoid taking possession of coke that it did not want by paying a fee—in effect, buying its way out of a contractual minimum. The fee covered at least some of the cost the refinery would bear in disposing of its coke in some other way or shutting down its coker for a period of time. Other contracts contained pricing terms with volume discounts, which encouraged aluminum producers to place larger orders to the extent they could. The higher per-unit price paid for small orders indirectly compensated a refinery for the need to dispose of coke in other ways when purchases were too small to exhaust the refinery's backlog.

The contracts between refineries and aluminum companies reflect the tradeoff between the aluminum companies ensuring a return on the refineries' asset-specific investments and avoiding a situation in which the aluminum companies would bear the cost of unloading unwanted coke if demand for aluminum fell. While we cannot say that each contract was joint-value maximizing, in broad strokes they struck compromises that were consistent with that characterization. Each party bore a risk that it would lose out, but the result was the construction of a coking unit that produced products providing an upside to each party as well.

Here it is instructive to look at the deal between PetroVietnam and BP, under which BP drilled a gas well off the coast of Vietnam and agreed to deliver gas to Vietnam's state-owned energy company. The only potential buyer of gas from the well was PetroVietnam. The gas would be delivered through a pipeline from BP's wellhead to a facility owned by PetroVietnam, which would distribute the gas to its customers. While PetroVietnam was obligated to buy all the gas the well produced, the contract provided a degree of flexibility in the timing of its purchases.

To explain the arrangement, some facts about natural gas production will be helpful. First, the rate at which gas is extracted from a well affects the total amount of gas that can be extracted over the life of the well. For every well, there is a minimum and a maximum amount of gas that can be extracted per day without impairing the well's long-term productivity. Engineers perform tests when a well is drilled to estimate the total volume of gas in the well, which allows them to set minimum and maximum daily extraction levels. Within those parameters, the rate at which gas is extracted can vary without affecting the total productivity of the well. Second, after a well is drilled, gas flows naturally. But because wells are equipped with mechanisms to control the rate at which gas flows, a well operator can vary the amount of gas it delivers. Third, storage of gas requires an infrastructure of above-ground or below-ground storage facilities, which are expensive to build and maintain.

In the PetroVietnam-BP deal, there was no quantity adjustment with respect to the *total* amount of gas supplied over the term of the agreement. PetroVietnam was required to purchase all the gas in the well. If it did not, gas would be wasted, creating a cost that one or both of the companies would have to absorb. The agreement did, however, provide PetroVietnam with a degree of flexibility regarding the quantity of gas it took on a daily and yearly basis. This allowed PetroVietnam to respond to fluctuations in demand from its customers. PetroVietnam was required to take at least the minimum quantity of gas on a daily basis that was necessary to maintain the well's long-term productivity. And in each full year of the contract, PetroVietnam was required to purchase a minimum total amount of gas—a quantity greater than the sum of daily minimum amounts. This annual minimum purchase requirement shortened the time it took to deplete the well and increased the present value of the well to BP. Within the physical limit, however, PetroVietnam could pay for gas in one year and defer taking delivery until a later year. Any gas that PetroVietnam took in a later year, but paid for earlier, was referred to as "make-up gas." In addition, if PetroVietnam took more gas than the annual minimum in a given year, then it could apply that additional gas—"carry forward gas"—to a later year's minimum. But, PetroVietnam still had to take an amount of gas each day that was within the minimum and maximum physical limits of the well.

Thus, while PetroVietnam was required to purchase all gas in the well at a rate that maximized the well's productivity and provided BP with cash flows that amounted to an agreed-upon present value, PetroVietnam had flexibility to shift deliveries across time periods as it experienced changes in its customers' demand. This flexibility alleviated pressure on PetroVietnam's limited gas storage facilities and allowed it to make the most out of its purchases. PetroVietnam's flexibility was costless to BP. The quantity-adjustment provisions of the deal were thus joint-value-maximizing.

Another deal where quantity adjustments had to be anticipated was the one between TestCo and SemiCo, introduced in Chapter 5. As described there, TestCo is a privately held company with a new proprietary technology for testing advanced semiconductors, and SemiCo is a large, publicly held semiconductor manufacturer that was developing a new line of semiconductors. To secure a lucrative contract to produce testers for SemiCo's new line of semiconductors, TestCo would have to build a new factory with customized equipment. SemiCo, therefore, had to provide TestCo with assurance that it would purchase enough testers to justify that asset-specific investment. And on the other side of the deal, because the testers would be essential to SemiCo's semiconductors, SemiCo needed assurance that it would have the quantity of testers it needed. Any interruption in supply would delay production, with potentially devastating effect on SemiCo's business. We described in Chapter 5 how a limited second-source arrangement provided assurance to SemiCo that it would have the testers it needed.

But how was TestCo's investment in the new plant and customized equipment protected? SemiCo could not be sure of the quantity of testers it would need or how quickly sales would ramp up. So, if SemiCo were to guarantee a quantity of purchases, there would be a danger that it would buy testers that it could not use. Nonetheless, SemiCo had to provide some degree of assurance to TestCo. SemiCo agreed to a minimum purchase commitment and further committed that it would purchase at least 85 percent of its needs from TestCo (with the rest coming from the second source discussed in Chapter 5). The parties further agreed that TestCo could devote some of the plant's unused capacity to producing testers for other semiconductor manufacturers. SemiCo would communicate its order flow to TestCCO nine months in advance on a continuous basis. TestCo was required to reserve manufacturing capacity for that volume of testers, and to deliver up to that volume of testers to SemiCo. Unreserved capacity could be used for other testers. But SemiCo would place actual orders only one month in advance, and it was not required to order as many testers as it had projected months earlier.

These commitments opened up vulnerabilities for each party. SemiCo had an incentive to inflate its projections to ensure an adequate supply, which made TestCo vulnerable to having idle capacity. SemiCo, in turn, was vulnerable if its nine-month projections turned out to be too low, and TestCo could not produce the volume it needed. To respond to these vulnerabilities, the supply contract further stated that SemiCo must exercise "commercially reasonable" judgment in making its projections, and that TestCo must make "commercially reasonable" efforts to meet Semi-Co's purchasing requirements above the amounts projected. As we will discuss in Chapter 8, legal enforcement of those vague commitments would be uncertain. Nonetheless, SemiCo and TestCo had good reason to maintain a good working relationship, so legal enforcement may not have been the point.

The quantity-adjustment terms of the SemiCo-TestCo deal were similar to those in deals between the oil refineries and aluminum companies, in that each reflected a tradeoff between providing sufficient assurance to support an asset-specific investment and sharing the risk of future demand. In each, the assurance was apparently sufficient to have the asset-specific facility built. Presumably, the upside of that investment was high enough to justify the downside. In its deal with PetroVietnam, BP got complete assurance that it would sell all gas in its well. PetroVietnam was probably quite certain that there would be sufficient demand for that gas. Moreover, there was no other potential buyer of the gas, so it had little choice but to buy all the gas—or pay for wasted gas. The flexibility it had with respect to the timing of its purchases, however, was valuable.

Price Adjustment

Parties typically enter into a long-term contract for reasons other than maintaining a fixed price for a product. Generally, at least one side wants the price to change over time, and in most situations, both should want that. Price adjustments can be important in keeping the deal attractive to the parties. They can reduce the likelihood that one or the other party has more attractive options elsewhere, which can result in a party attempting to find a way out of the deal.

Cost-Plus Pricing to Induce Product Development

When a contract involves a product that the parties expect to improve over the term of the contract, both parties will see value in allowing the seller to recoup the cost of the product's further development to protect its profit margin. Otherwise, the seller would have little incentive to make the improvements. A classic example of this is cost-plus pricing in military contracts. When the US government enters into a contract for the development of a new aircraft, for example, much of the cost that the defense contractor will incur and many details of the aircraft are unknown. The military and the contractor agree to a price adjustment that gives the contractor a specified margin above its costs.

Cost-plus pricing is common but it does have serious drawbacks.[2] Well-known problems include a lack of incentive for the seller to manage costs, difficulty in attributing fixed costs when sales volume is uncertain, the need for the buyer to monitor the seller's production and accounting for costs, and the need for the seller to give the buyer confidential information about its production processes and costs.

Tracking Market Prices to Promote Cooperation
and Avoid Counterproductive Conduct

A second, and analytically more interesting, objective of a price adjustment mechanism is to have the contract price track the market price of the product being sold. There are two reasons that parties may want to do this. First, if a gap opens up between the market price and the contract price of the product at some point during the term of the contract, the buyer or the seller might exploit that difference to the detriment of its counterparty. Imagine a requirements contract in which the seller agrees to sell the buyer whatever volume of goods the buyer needs. If at some point in the term of the contract, the market price of the good is higher than the contract price, the buyer could buy more under the contract than it otherwise would buy. Depending on the nature of the good, the buyer might find ways to use the extra goods in its own business—in the case of an intermediate good, for example, changing factor proportions in its own production—or sell the excess purchases on the open market (if that is permitted under the contract). Either response is counterproductive. To the extent the seller foresees this possibility, it will, in theory at least, charge a higher price at the outset. If the parties can design a mechanism that prevents such conduct, they should do so.

A second reason parties may want the contract price of the product to track its market price is that, if the market price diverges significantly from the contract price for a substantial period of time, one side or the other will have an incentive to get out of the contract. Especially if the point of having a long-term contract is to protect an asset-specific investment, it is important to negotiate a deal that will last.

In Oliver Hart's model of "reference points," mentioned in Chapter 5, price is a key example of a reference point. So long as a buyer is happy paying an agreed-upon price and complying with other basic terms set out in a contract, Hart theorizes that the parties will expand their cooperation in other ways—ways that could not have been specified in advance but that are mutually advantageous. If such a basic term becomes unattractive, however, cooperation will cease, at a minimum, and the party bearing the cost may find a way out of the deal. A party seeking a way out of a deal will probably not breach the contract outright, since doing so could result in a lawsuit and a damage award. But it may make life difficult for its counterparty because it wants to pressure the counterparty to renegotiate. There may be gaps or ambiguities in a contract that can be exploited for this purpose. For example, the quality of a product may be imprecisely defined, allowing the seller to deliver subpar products. Conversely, a buyer may claim that a product is subpar and refuse delivery or exploit a right to return goods. Such behavior is collectively costly. If there is a mechanism that can keep a gap from opening up between the contract and market price of the product being exchanged, the parties should use it.

Adjusting a contract price to track a market price can be difficult. One apparently simple way is to use a price index, such as the Consumer Price Index or Producer Price Index published by the US Bureau of Labor Statistics. There are many such indices and subindices available. But a ready-made index might not track the market price of the particular product being sold. To the extent it does not, the problem of counterproductive behavior remains. Alternatively, the parties could find a similar product available on the market with a publicly available price that correlates with the market price of the product being sold, or they could create an index of multiple products expected to correlate with the market price of their product. The product being sold, however, may be unique, in which case using other products to index the contract price will be imperfect. Adjustments can be made that improve the fit, which is well worth doing, but precision will be difficult to achieve.

A well-known indexing failure occurred in a contract between the Essex Group and Alcoa of America, analyzed in detail by Victor Goldberg.[3] This contract became the subject of litigation that still appears in contract law textbooks. But the legal treatment of the contract is not the issue on which we focus here. The Essex Group built an aluminum wire and cable fabrication plant near Alcoa's aluminum smelter in Warrick, Indiana. Prior to building the plant, Essex entered into a roughly twenty-year contract with Alcoa, under which Alcoa would smelt and deliver molten aluminum to Essex's nearby plant. Taking delivery of molten aluminum from Alcoa's nearby smelter saved Essex transportation and other costs. The plant was an asset-specific investment. To justify construction of the plant, Essex needed assurance that Alcoa would provide molten aluminum at a price consistent with its own ability to sell aluminum wire and cable over the course of the contract. Essex therefore needed a price adjustment to the initially agreed price of fifteen cents per pound of molten aluminum.

The parties took the wrong approach from the start—and then implemented that approach poorly to boot. They constructed their own price index based on Alcoa's cost, not the market price of aluminum. This was a fundamental mistake. It was Essex that primarily needed the protection—specifically, assurance that the price it paid Alcoa would be consistent with the price it could charge for aluminum wire and cable. The index, however, was poorly designed to accomplish that objective. In the end, it failed miserably. Yet, as it turned out, it was Alcoa that bore the cost of the misconceived index, not Essex (at least until Alcoa convinced a court to come to its rescue).

It was a mistake for Alcoa and Essex to base the price adjustment on Alcoa's costs. But the adjustment even failed to do that effectively. The adjustment mechanism separated the initial fifteen-cent-per-pound price into two parts: a ten-cent "production charge" and a five-cent "demand charge," and inexplicably failed to index the five-cent demand charge. The ten-cent production charge was divided into three components: a three-cent nonlabor cost, a three-cent labor cost, and four cents of profit. The labor cost was indexed to Alcoa's actual labor cost at its Warwick plant. The nonlabor cost was indexed to the industrial component of the US Bureau of Labor Statistics' wholesale price index (now known as the Producer Price Index). And the profit component was not indexed—again, inexplicably. So, in sum, three-fifths of the price (nine of fifteen cents) was not indexed.

Furthermore, as would later be discovered, the three-cent nonlabor cost was indexed poorly. Alcoa's expenditures on energy made up most of its nonlabor cost, since it needed to heat alumina to 1475°F to extract aluminum. As a result of the 1973 oil crisis, energy prices rose 300 percent, while the industrial component of the wholesale price index less than doubled. Not surprisingly, the index failed to track Alcoa's cost. About midway through the twenty-year contract, Essex was paying Alcoa twenty-five cents per pound, and Alcoa's cost of smelting the aluminum for Essex was thirty-five cents per pound. So, Alcoa was losing ten cents per pound in out-of-pocket cost.

More importantly, however, aluminum was selling on the market for seventy-three cents per pound, so Alcoa faced forty-eight cents per pound in opportunity cost. This was in part due to the failure of the index to track costs, but in addition, during the term of the contract, demand for aluminum rose, so even if the cost-based adjustment had been good, the contract price would have been lower than the market price.

Essex, the party that had made the asset-specific investment—and therefore the party that needed protection—made out well in this deal. But things could have gone differently with the index it agreed to use. If the market price of aluminum had fallen as a result of reduced demand, Essex would have been stuck with higher costs than its competitors.

As it turned out, it was Alcoa that bore the cost of change. It had a twenty-year commitment to sell aluminum at a price far below market. Alcoa therefore sought to get out of the contract. Presumably, the terms were such that there were no gaps to exploit, so instead Alcoa sued under the legal doctrine of *mutual mistake*, *impracticability*, and *frustration*. In a decision that most commentators believe was incorrect, a court bailed Alcoa out of its problem and reformulated the contract so that Alcoa was guaranteed a small profit.

Other Ways to Track Market Prices

Other contractual mechanisms that have the potential to keep the contract price of a product in line with its market price include a *most-favored-nation* provision, a *matching right*, and a *renegotiation right*. All have serious flaws, especially in the context of an asset-specific investment, but each can be workable in some cases.

A *most-favored-nation* provision provides that, over the course of a long-term contract, a seller may charge a buyer no more than the amount it charges other buyers for the same product. If market prices change over, say, a twenty-year contract, those changing prices will appear in the seller's later deals with other buyers, which would mean the contract price would be adjusted to match prices. This mechanisms works, of course, only if a seller sells similar products to similarly situated buyers on a reasonably regular basis. When an asset-specific investment is involved, this is unlikely to be the case. TestCo, however, agreed to this arrangement with SemiCo, committing to charge TestCo a price no higher than the price it charged for "substantially similar testers." Since the testers that TestCo produced for SemiCo were unique to SemiCo's new semiconductor, it is unclear how effective this commitment was. But since TestCo's deal with SemiCo was essential to its reputation, it was unlikely that TestCo would treat SemiCo badly.

A second mechanism is a *matching right*. The way it works is that either a buyer or a seller has a right to seek a competing deal from a third party. Its counterparty then has a right to match the third-party offer, in which case the relationship continues. If the counterparty chooses not to match, the deal may be terminated. If third-party offers are readily available, a matching right can be a reasonable means of having a contract price track the market price. Third-party offers should reflect the current market price of the product being sold. But there are at least two potential drawbacks. First, if a contract involves a unique product or service, or it comes from a uniquely advantageous physical location, there may be no third party in a position to make an offer. Second, if a third party would bear any significant cost in preparing an offer, it may decline to do so if it knows that another party holds a right to match that offer. Unless the third party has reason to believe its offer will not be matched, why bother? The third party will be even more hesitant to make a bid if the party with the matching right has relevant information that the third party lacks. If the third party's offer succeeds, it may be because it was unaware of something important.

Yet another way to keep contract prices in line with market prices is a right to *renegotiate*. The renegotiation right might be triggered by specified events, or might call for a price to be revisited at specified time intervals—say, every five years. This approach to tracking market prices is also imperfect—substantially more so than a matching right—and it is not commonly used when an asset-specific investment is involved. First, if there is no market for the product being sold, a renegotiation right will not be a means of tracking a market price. It will be a way to allow either party to decide it is better off without the deal, irrespective of the availability of alternative deals for the same product. Second, if there is an imbalance of potential buyers and sellers in the market, a renegotiation may not yield a competitive market price. Imagine, for example, a situation in which there is a single potential seller for a product and multiple buyers. Rather than maintaining a long-term deal with a current market price, a renegotiation right may instead convert a long-term contract into a short-term contract.

7

EXITING A LONG-TERM DEAL

The terms under which a deal can be terminated can be as critical to transaction design as the terms that govern its performance. From the narrow perspective of one party, there is often value in having an unconditional right to terminate when a deal is no longer beneficial. In a long-term supply contract, for example, a buyer may want freedom to stop making purchases if it no longer needs what is being supplied, or if it finds a better deal elsewhere. If the supplier can easily replace the lost revenue with sales to others, the buyer's termination may be costless. And if it will take time for a counterparty to replace its lost sales, a simple solution may be to require advance notice. But, if the supplier has made an asset-specific investment to produce what it is selling, the buyer's termination will impose costs on the supplier—it will lose the value of its investment. In other circumstances, termination may be costly to a party initiating the termination. A buyer that contributed to the development of the supplier's product will lose the value of that investment if it simply walks away. In this chapter, we address exit mechanisms that have the potential to preserve the value that parties create during the course of their relationship.

In any deal requiring an asset-specific investment, the extent to which a party is willing to make that investment will depend in part on termination terms. To the extent a party anticipates its own need to exit, it will hesitate to invest unless it knows it can retain the value of the investment when it exits. And to the extent a party expects that its counterparty may exit, it will hesitate to invest unless it is protected from losing the value of its investment in that event. If a significant asset-specific investment will be valuable to the deal, the parties may either need to accept constraints on their right to terminate, or find a way to ensure that, if one does terminate, each will retain the value of its investment. Recall, for example, PetroVietnam's agreement to purchase natural gas from BP for at least twenty years, discussed in Chapter 6. If PetroVietnam were able to terminate that deal, BP would have a stranded gas well off the coast of Vietnam with no alternative buyer of its gas. BP, therefore, did not grant PetroVietnam a right to terminate. In other situations, more flexible exit mechanisms can be devised that allow exit while preserving and thereby encouraging asset-specific investment.

Sometimes, however, even sophisticated parties fail to put exit terms into their initial agreement. The result can be unpleasant, as a group of investors found when they bought Philadelphia's main newspaper, the *Inquirer,* for $55 million in 2012. George Norcross, Lewis Katz, and some smaller investors expected to remain partners for a long time, and their partnership agreement did not include an exit mechanism. By January 2014 they were openly feuding about the newspaper's future and, unable to resolve their differences, agreed to sell the business. An outside buyer proved impossible to find; the most interested party was Ray Perelman, then ninety-seven years old and the father of famed dealmaker Ronald Perelman, but he soon backed out. The only way the parties could terminate their relationship—short of simply shutting down the newspaper at great cost—was for one of the main partners, Norcross or Katz, to buy out the other.

Not surprisingly, Norcross and Katz disagreed about the process that would determine who would sell, who would buy, and at what price. Norcross advocated an open-outcry, ascending auction: the bidding would start low, and Norcross and Katz would each bid to buy the company until only one of them was left standing. Katz advocated a single-round, sealed-bid auction: Norcross and Katz would each submit a price at which he would buy the company, the envelopes would be opened, and the party that submitted the highest bid would buy out the other. With no agreement on a process, Norcross and Katz went to court.[1]

The court had to pick an exit mechanism because the parties had failed to do so themselves. After trial, the court ordered an open-outcry auction between Katz and Norcross. The auction took place in downtown Philadelphia. The bidding started at $77 million, and each side had ten minutes to increase its bid by at least $1 million. In the end, Katz won, with a bid of $88 million. Presumably, Katz valued the newspaper most highly, and Norcross reaped some of the benefit of his valuation. But there was a lot of ill will, expense, and distraction for the newspaper along the way.

The remainder of this section focuses on the preferable scenario where parties to a deal negotiate exit rights in their initial agreement. We will explore the two possible avenues highlighted by the *Inquirer* example: requiring one partner to sell to the other, and allowing either partner to sell to a third party. Most of the discussion uses the setting of a business in which asset- or relationship-specific investments have been made by one or both partners and they are therefore dependent on one another. But the mechanisms apply to any other setting in which there is asset-specific investment and a need to contemplate exit.

Where one partner must sell to the other, there are three central issues that an exit mechanism must address: first, whether one or both partners will be assured of an exit; second, whether the exiting party will be able to sell its interest at a price that reflects the value of its interest; and third, whether the partner that remains with the business will be vulnerable to a loss in value as a result of its counterparty's exit. Where a sale to a third party is contemplated, the same issues are present, along with two additional issues: whether the party that remains will have any say in who its new partner will be;

and whether a party can be forced to sell its interest. These goals are often mutually incompatible. The exit mechanisms described below strike different balances between them.

Sale from One Partner to Another

In some situations, partners in a deal involving an asset- or relationship-specific investment can foresee the possibility that no third party will buy the interest of either partner if one chooses to exit—at least not at a price that reflects the value of the partner's interest. This means the partners will have only each other as potential buyers, as in the case of the *Inquirer*. In this scenario, the partners need to consider how much assurance each can give the other that a buyout will occur, and how the price of a departing partner's interest will be set. There are a few contractual mechanisms that address these issues, but with any of them, the solvency and liquidity of the parties at the time of a sale will influence their effectiveness.

Commitment to Negotiate (Or Consider) "In Good Faith"

One approach to an interparty sale is simply to provide in a contract that, if one party wants to sell its interest to the other, the parties will "negotiate in good faith" or "consider an offer in good faith." When the time comes for a sale, however, the parties may well have different views regarding what constitutes good faith—and different views on how much value should be placed on each other's interest in the company. If one side rejects the other's offer, they may have to litigate both these questions, and the outcome of that litigation will be uncertain. A party contemplating exit under a good-faith standard, therefore, would have little assurance of a sale to its partner and little certainty, if a sale did occur, of receiving what it considered to be the right price.

A few years ago, the Carlyle Group, a private equity firm, bought the water system of Missoula, Montana. Carlyle's purchase of Missoula's water system was an asset-specific investment: its value depended on the city's cooperation in facilitating its residents' purchase of water. Missoula, at the same time, was dependent on Carlyle as the supplier of its water. The city would have liked to own the water system itself but had insufficient cash on hand to make an offer to buy the system from its then-owner, a private individual. The city did, however, obtain an agreement from Carlyle that Carlyle would "consider any offer in good faith" if the city wished to make an offer in the future. Mayor John Engen told the press that he wanted a stronger commitment, but the agreement to "consider in good faith" was the best he could get. And from Carlyle's perspective, a "consider in good faith" commitment was a cheap give—indeed, why *wouldn't* Carlyle consider in good faith any offer that Missoula (or any other prospective buyer) made? Private equity firms are always sellers, at the right price. This was an interesting twist on the exit scenario in that it was a means by which the city could induce an exit as opposed to one in which Carlyle would initiate an exit. Nonetheless, the underlying issues were the same. How much assurance would the city have that it could buy out Carlyle at a price it could accept?

A few years later, when Missoula indeed made Carlyle an offer to buy the water system, Carlyle hired outside advisors to evaluate it and ultimately sent a letter to Mayor Engen documenting why it declined to accept the city's offer. The fact that, shortly thereafter, Carlyle sold the water system to a third party for approximately 50 percent more than Missoula's offer confirmed that the city's offer had been low. Missoula nevertheless took Carlyle to arbitration, arguing that Carlyle had not considered its offer in good faith—hoping to benefit from the vagueness of the term.[2] The arbitrator had no trouble concluding that Carlyle had satisfied its obligation to "consider in good faith" any offer from the city; both because the obligation was minimal at best, and because Carlyle had engaged in a significant process to consider the offer.

As the Missoula-Carlyle deal illustrates, the use of a vague standard in an exit mechanism, as opposed to a hard rule, can be problematic. It does little to reduce uncertainties around the possibility of exit and it creates the potential for costly litigation. Faced with such uncertainties, the parties will have less incentive to make asset-specific investments while working together, or to enter into a deal in the first place. Exit mechanisms that are rule-based avoid these disincentives—but as we will see next, they come with problems of their own.

Third-Party Appraisal

A relatively simple process that avoids the uncertainty of a mere good-faith negotiation commitment is an agreement that, if a party wants to exit, the business will be appraised by a professional appraiser and sold to its counterparty. The parties could further agree to a mandatory sale at the appraised price. Alternatively, the contract could state that the sale would only proceed subject to the agreement of both parties, but this, of course, would not assure the possibility of exit.

Under some circumstances, an appraisal may not be as simple as it appears. Let's say the exiting partner had been contributing important skills, and its exit will reduce the value of the company. In that case, it is unclear what that partner should receive. If ownership had been fifty-fifty, should the buyout price be half the company's pre-exit value, or should the price reflect the disproportionate contribution of the exiting party? There is no right answer to this question. Ideally, the parties would negotiate this and specify an approach to valuation at the outset or during the course of their relationship, keeping in mind that they want to encourage each other to make optimal investments while they work together.

Reliance on a professional appraisal also raises the issue of how the parties will select the appraiser. How can they be assured of an appraiser's competence and lack of bias? One approach is to provide that the parties will work together to select an appraiser from a reputable firm that knows their industry. Or, if there is an accounting firm or an investment bank that both parties trust, the agreement can provide that the appraisal will be done by someone from that firm who has had no prior contact with either party. This approach can still result in the parties disagreeing, and failing to select an appraiser, finding themselves in litigation, but it is commonly used.

Another approach is for the parties to agree that each will select an appraiser, and that those two appraisers will then select a third. Their agreement might further provide that the selling price would be the average of the three appraisals or would match the one in the middle. Hiring three appraisers is, of course, more expensive than hiring one, but if the value of the business is large enough, the expense can be justified by the reduced risk of an errant valuation.

Yet another approach is for both parties to perform their own valuations and give them to a mutually trusted appraiser to judge which is most accurate. If the appraiser must make a choice between only the two options provided, there will be incentive for each party to be reasonable in its valuation. This method is a variation of *baseball-style* arbitration, so named because an arbitrator in a professional baseball salary dispute must choose between the two offers proposed by the team and the player.

Buyout at a Formula Price

A third approach to an inter-partner sale is for the partners to agree in advance that each is obligated to buy out the other, upon request, according to a formula—for example, ten or twenty times average annual profits over the past three years. This approach provides assurance of exit (again, with the caveat that the buying side must be sufficiently liquid and solvent when the time comes). But coming up with a formula at the time the partners are entering into the deal is not easy. When the time comes to use the formula, the resulting price could well be out of line with the company's value—to the detriment of either party. A formula based on recent profits, for example, may not be an appropriate way to gauge the value of the business. It could be that, in the months leading up to the moment when a partner wants to exit, the company has made a strategic decision to sacrifice short-term profits and make a valuable long-term investment. Or perhaps at the time of the exit profits are rising and are expected to increase further. In either case, the average of recent years' profits does not constitute a good measure of the company's present value. A contract can spell out a customized, complex formula but the general problem remains that, especially when exit may not occur for many years, coming up with a reliable way to measure value will be difficult.

Buy-Sell Agreement

Another mechanism that might (or might not) work is a *buy-sell* agreement—sometimes called a *put-call*, or, for reasons that are not entirely clear, a *shootout* or even a *Texas shootout* clause. In a buy-sell agreement, the parties agree when they enter into a deal that either side can at any time make an offer to buy out the other's shares at a price it names. The interesting wrinkle is that any such offer to buy is simultaneously an offer to *sell*. The party that receives the offer can choose either to sell its interest or to buy out the offeror's interest at the specified price. Thus the party making the initial offer must stand ready either to become the sole owner of the business or to give up its entire interest in it. So perhaps it is not accurate to include the buy-sell provision in a discussion of exit mechanisms, since the result will not necessarily be that the party triggering the buy-sell leaves the business. On the other hand, if that party finds itself in the unwanted position of owning the entire business, it can always try to sell.

The beauty of the buy-sell is that the mechanism forces the party making a buyout offer to name a price that it considers reasonable, since it could be a buyer or a seller at that price. If the offeror's price is too low, the offeree may buy out the offeror at that low price. If it is high, the offeror may have to buy out its partner at the high price. Under the right conditions, the offer will be just right.

A buy-sell, however, is a good fit for a deal only under limited circumstances in which there is symmetry between the parties in three respects. First, both parties' involvement must be of equal value to the business, each party must value the business equally as sole owner, and each must be equally interested in becoming a sole owner. As noted above, sometimes one party's involvement is more valuable to a business than the other's. If the party that contributes more value wants to exit, it will have to offer a price that is, at most, equal to the value of the business without his involvement. Otherwise, its partner will choose to sell rather than buy. So, in that situation, the party wanting to exit will not be able to extract the value it places on its share of the business. Second, each party must have liquidity sufficient to buy out the other. Without sufficient liquidity, a party may have to sell out cheaply, either because it cannot initiate the buy-sell at a price at which it cannot buy, or because its partner may take advantage of the situation and make a lowball offer that is still above what the illiquid partner can afford. The third condition is that the parties must have similar information regarding the business, so that their valuations are at least roughly in line. Otherwise, the more informed party can take advantage of the less informed party.

In a situation well-suited to a buy-sell, this mechanism should, in theory at least, provide some assurance that a party wishing to exit will be able to do so at a roughly fair price, and also that a party that wishes to buy out its partner will be able to do so. To exit, a party would offer a price slightly below the fair price, and a party wishing to buy out its partner would offer a price slightly above the fair price. In practice, however, the very different outcomes that can follow the exercise of a buy-sell clause are a source of added uncertainty.

An example of a misconceived effort to employ a buy-sell mechanism was in a joint venture between the apparel maker Levi Strauss & Co. and a Boston-based company called Designs, Inc., whose business was to operate brand-specific retail outlets under agreements with apparel marketers. Designs had been selling Levi's apparel for several years. The objective of the joint venture was to create a chain of high-profile shops called "The Original Levi's Store" that, on top of generating retail sales, would serve as flagships promoting Levi's brand image.

This would be an asset-specific investment for Designs, but not for Levi Strauss. Designs would convert retail stores it was already operating under its own name into Original Levi's Stores, devoted solely to Levi Strauss products. Designs would be able to return these stores to their old business only at substantial cost. Levi Strauss operated its own retail stores in other parts of the country and was able to run these stores on its own, but it chose to partner with Designs because Designs was known to be a well-run retail operation. Levi Strauss saw Designs as a company that could help with the branding it was trying to accomplish.

Levi Strauss and Designs entered into their joint venture with every expectation that they would remain in business together for a long time. But they also recognized that a situation might arise in which one or the other might want to exit. As an exit mechanism, they chose a buy-sell.

The buy-sell, however, was a bad fit for this deal. The necessary conditions were not present—none of them. Designs was the party that needed assurance that it would recoup its asset-specific investment if either it or Levi Strauss chose to exit. But the buy-sell provided little assurance to Designs. First, the business would be more valuable under Levi Strauss's sole ownership than Designs' sole ownership, because Levi's would reap the benefit of the stores serving as a marketing vehicle for its sales generally and Levi's could manage the stores toward that end. In addition, under Levi's ownership, the supply relationship would be consolidated, whereas under Designs ownership Designs would be reliant on Levi Strauss. Second, Designs could well have less liquidity than Levi's. And third, Levi's view of the worldwide jeans and denim market may have given it better information about the value of the joint venture than Designs had. For all these reasons, if Levi Strauss chose to buy out Designs, it would be able to trigger the buy-sell process by offering a price equal to Design's valuation as a sole owner—a value that would have been below the value of Design's share of the joint venture, and below Levi Strauss's valuation of the business as a sole owner. Furthermore, if Designs wanted to exit and had to initiate the buy-sell process, it would have to offer that same, relatively low valuation in order to avoid having to buy out Levi's at too high a price.[3]

As it turned out, the joint venture terminated by mutual agreement, and the buy-sell was never tested.

Sale to a Third Party

Sometimes, partners in a business foresee the possibility of selling their interests in the business, whether separately or together, to a third party—a situation not addressed by the exit mechanisms discussed above, where one partner sells its interest to the other. Typically in such scenarios, there are three conflicting desires or concerns in play. First, the parties want substantial freedom to exit via sale to a third party. Neither wants its partner to have the power to prevent that sale. Second, neither wants to find itself in a position in which it is forced to sell. And third, if only one party favors selling to a third party, the other wants to have a say in who its new business partner will be. These objectives conflict with one another; one or both parties will have to give in on one or more of them. Exit mechanisms that govern sales to third parties must strike a balance between these three concerns. Potential mechanisms include veto rights, black lists, rights of first refusal, rights of first offer, drag-along rights, tag-along rights, and combinations of any of these.

Veto Rights and Black Lists

One approach to balancing the interests of an exiting partner and the interests of the remaining partner is to give the latter a limited *veto right*. The limits on the veto right, however, are important and must be carefully negotiated and circumscribed. The concern with a veto right is not only that exit may become impossible, but also that the partner with the veto right may use the right to extract gains from the partner that needs to exit. A compromise is for the parties to negotiate *black lists* at the time of the agreement—identifying the parties to which an exiting party may not sell. Each partner would list, for example, competitors and others with which that partner does not want to work while still allowing a reasonable possibility for other potential buyers to emerge.

Rights of First Refusal

Another way to structure an exit right is to allow a partner to sell its interest to a third party, but only after it gives the partner that remains an opportunity to purchase that interest on the terms to which the third-party has agreed. This is referred to as a *right of first refusal* (RoFR). The way it works is that the exiting partner, having identified an interested third party, proceeds to negotiate a sale to that party. The terms of the sale they negotiate need not be fully specified in a final agreement; a term sheet typically suffices. The exiting partner then shares the terms of that offer with the remaining partner, who can choose to buy out the exiting partner on those terms. If the remaining party declines to match the offer on the table, the exiting partner is free to sell to the third party.

At first glance, a RoFR appears to strike a reasonable balance between the interest of an exiting partner and the interest of the partner that remains with the business. It appears to allow exit at a fair price while giving the remaining partner a way to avoid getting stuck with an unwanted new partner. But it may not be as reasonable as it first appears. First, the right it grants is rather meaningless if the remaining partner lacks the liquidity to exercise it. Second, consider the RoFR from the perspective of the third party interested in buying the exiting partner's interest. Presumably, the third party will ask whether a RoFR exists. If it does, the third party might be hesitant to embark on an expensive process of due diligence, valuation, and negotiation, knowing it could all be for naught if the RoFR is exercised. Depending on the third party's expectation of how likely the RoFR holder is to exercise its right, and how costly it will be to prepare and negotiate an offer, the third party might choose not to bother. Furthermore, the third party will understand that, in effect, it will be bidding against an insider for the exiting partner's interests, and the insider could well have better information about the business's value. Looking at these prospects, the third party could find itself in a "heads you win, tails I lose" situation: if the RoFR is exercised, it will have wasted its time, and if the RoFR is not exercised, it will suspect it overpaid.

This is not to say that rights of first refusal always prevent sales to third parties. A third party might have sound reasons to place a value on the business greater than the RoFR holder's valuation, perhaps reflecting its own idiosyncratic interests. A theater lover, for example, with a lot of cash might be willing to pay more for a theater company than a financial buyer without that particular interest. Likewise, a third party might willingly pay a premium for a business that offers valuable synergies with another business it already operates. Such an enthusiastic buyer is also one that the remaining partner will more likely welcome. To that end, the third party might also meet with the RoFR holder and seek assurance that the right would not be exercised.

In general, however, RoFRs are viewed as putting a damper on third-party offers. RoFRs tend to be resisted by parties that foresee a need to exit a deal—and sought by parties that do not want their partners to sell to third parties.

Rights of First Offer

An alternative to a RoFR is a *right of first offer*, or RoFO. A RoFO requires an exiting partner first to make an offer to its partner. If the partner declines the offer, the exiting partner may then seek a third-party buyer, but only on the terms that the partner has turned down, or terms that are less attractive to a buyer.

A RoFO still puts the third party in the position of bidding against an insider that may be better informed. The third party will presumably ask whether there is a RoFO in place, and confirm that it was not exercised. So, the third party may well be deterred from making an offer. But the third party may inquire further and discover that the reason the RoFO was not exercised was unrelated to whether it was a good offer. And, in contrast to a bid in the context of a RoFR, the third party will know that, if it goes forward with due diligence and chooses to accept the offer, it will have a deal. RoFOs, therefore, do not deter third-party bids as much as ROFRs do, and for that reason they are more common than RoFRs. Where they are exercised as envisioned, they can be expected to yield a fair price.

Drag-Along and Tag-Along Rights

A *drag-along right* provides an exiting party with the right to force its partner to sell to a third party on the same terms to which the exiting partner agrees—to drag the partner into a sale. This right gives the exiting partner assurance that, if a third party to which it wants to sell is only interested in buying the entire company, it can do so.

If two partners value their business similarly, then a deal struck by the initiating party will be attractive to its partner as well, and the drag-along right does not disadvantage the partner that is dragged along. The drag-along right is thus value-maximizing. If, however, the exiting party is desperate to exit or values the business differently from its partner, the drag-along right could force the partner to sell at a price it considers less than fair.

A drag-along right gives an exiting party the right, but not the obligation, to force its partner to sell. Unless the partner has the right to join the exiting partner in a sale to a third party, that partner could find itself left behind with an unwanted partner. A *tag-along right* addresses that situation by giving the non-initiating partner the right to sell on the same terms as the initiating partner. Drag-along and tag-along rights may coexist in a deal, or one or the other may be present alone.

Combining Exit Rights

When a private equity fund acquires shares in a company, the fund's managers know the fund will have to exit within several years. The terms of the fund's agreements with its investors provide that the fund will liquidate and distribute cash within about ten years of its formation. Exit from an investment in a portfolio company is thus nonnegotiable. In addition to an unencumbered right to exit, the fund will insist on drag-along rights with respect to the shares of other investors. If its best exit option is the sale of the entire company, it will want the freedom to sell other investors' shares along with its own.

The private equity fund has every reason to sell at the best price available. So, unless the fund is forced by the timing of its own liquidation to sell into a weak market, other shareholders should not be disadvantaged by the fund's exercise of drag-along rights. On the other hand, those shareholders may not want to be left behind with a new controlling shareholder not of their choosing. To avoid that outcome, they will often negotiate tag-along rights. The combination of drag-along and tag-along rights will generally be value-maximizing for the shareholders.

Paramount Studios and NBC employed an interesting combination of renewal rights in their contract for the hit TV show *Frasier*. Their contract provided that NBC would carry the show for three years and, when its three-year term ended, the parties would follow an intricate process to negotiate renewal. These renewal rights amounted to exit rights. First, there would be a thirty-day exclusive negotiating period. If they did not reach agreement by the end of the thirty days, Paramount would submit a *last offer* to NBC. If NBC accepted this last offer, then they had a deal. If NBC rejected the last offer, then Paramount could shop the show to other potential buyers. If Paramount reached a deal with someone else that was *less* favorable to itself than the last offer (for example, if the price was lower), NBC had the right to match that deal and keep the show. But if Paramount reached a deal with a third party that was *more* favorable to Paramount than the last offer (for example, a higher price), NBC had no match right. Putting it all together, these exit rights amounted to a right of first offer backed up by a partial right of first refusal—partial because NBC's match right would come into play only if a third party offered a better deal to Paramount than the deal that NBC had turned down. In other words, NBC got a second shot only at a deal more favorable to it than the last offer it rejected.

This combination was not as favorable to NBC as a pure RoFR. Paramount was free to sell the show for an amount greater than its last offer to NBC. Unlike a pure RoFR, a third party would not be deterred from making such an offer, except to the extent it knew it would be outbidding NBC. On the other hand, the combination was more favorable to NBC than the RoFO alone. The partial RoFR at a price below the last offer would probably deter third-party bids, and if there were a bid, NBC would still be able to buy the show on the third party's terms.

As it turned out, Viacom, the owner of Paramount, bought CBS, which was the primary alternative to NBC as a buyer of the show. So Paramount, in effect, negotiated with itself for the show—an outcome that was not anticipated when the exit rights were negotiated, but that caused no harm.

As another example, recall the deal between the regional sports network and the baseball team described in Chapter 5. Over the course of that deal, the network would make substantial investments in developing a market for the team and its broadcasts. Those investments would be asset-specific to the team. The team, of course, wanted to encourage the investments, and the network wanted to be able to continue reaping rewards from its investments. The parties negotiated a twenty-year agreement, at the end of which the network would have a combination of renewal rights similar to those that NBC negotiated with Paramount. There was, however, one important difference: the network agreed to allow the team to buy out its renewal rights—that is, the team could make a payment to the network and be free to terminate the relationship. But the payment would be substantial, which reflected the value the network placed on the renewal rights—and indirectly, the value of is asset-specific investment. The buyout gave the team some flexibility to do something different if there were unexpected changes in the market or in the technological environment of local broadcasts.

Exit rights are important in supporting value-increasing incentives while parties are engaged in a deal, but they are also important because they can go wrong. When the Miami Dolphins football team brought in an investor, the family that owned the team made a serious mistake. Its granting of exit rights came back to haunt it when it sold the team.

The story begins in the mid-1970s, when Joe Robbie became the owner of the Miami Dolphins and went on, with legendary coach Don Shula, to build the team into a powerhouse. By 1990, the Miami

Dolphins could boast of being one of the most valuable teams in the NFL. Its value was estimated to be $145 million in 1993, when the average value of an NFL franchise was somewhere between $30 million and $40 million.

In 1987, Robbie built a new stadium, the Joe Robbie Stadium, that revolutionized the economics of professional sports. The stadium was designed to accommodate football, soccer, and baseball. And it was built with an innovation: luxury boxes, which have since become a common feature of stadiums.

It turned out that the stadium's revenues were insufficient to cover payments on its debt, so in 1990 Robbie brought in a partner who would contribute equity. That partner was Wayne Huizenga, a well-known Florida entrepreneur and longtime season-ticket holder. While Joe Robbie was negotiating an investment from Huizenga, Robbie passed away. His children continued the negotiations and eventually reached a deal. In exchange for a $70 million equity investment and an assumption of $45 million of existing debt on the stadium, Huizenga got a 50 percent share of the Joe Robbie Stadium, a 15 percent interest in the Dolphins, and an option to purchase an additional 10 percent of the Dolphins within five years.

Huizenga also got a right of first refusal. If the Robbies decided to sell their interest in the Dolphins, Huizenga had the right to match any offer they received from a third party. If Huizenga decided not to buy out the Robbies, then the Robbies could exercise a drag-along right and force Huizenga to sell on the same terms they accepted. This allowed the Robbies to sell 100 percent of the Dolphins to a third party.

Soon after Huizenga bought these interests in the Dolphins and Joe Robbie Stadium, Major League Baseball expanded into Florida, and Huizenga was granted a franchise for a new Florida team—the Florida Marlins. Joe Robbie Stadium would be the home stadium for the Marlins, as well. The details of the leases of the stadium to the Dolphins and the Marlins are not publicly known, but we can infer from the public record that having the Marlins play base-ball in Joe Robbie Stadium reduced the Dolphins' lease payments.

Within a few years, the Robbies concluded that, for their own financial reasons, they needed to sell their interests in the Dolphins and the stadium. The combination of the right of first refusal and the drag-along rights meant, in effect, that Wayne Huizenga would be either a buyer or a seller—a buyer of the Robbie interests in the Dolphins and the stadium, or a seller of his own interests to a third party. Whether he would be a buyer or a seller would depend on the price the Robbies were offered for their interests, which would be the price at which Huizenga could buy out the Robbies or sell to the third party along with the Robbies.

Despite the fact that the Dolphins franchise was among the most valuable sports franchises in the nation, and Joe Robbie Stadium was a state-of-the-art facility, few buyers stepped forward to make an offer. It was reported that, throughout all of the discussions between the Robbies and potential bidders, there was a single constant theme: Wayne Huizenga. Although not in the room, Wayne Huizenga was, by the account of one bidder, the single most important person in the deal.

Why was Huizenga important? Because his right of first refusal created a situation in which a third-party buyer would have to outbid him. If a third party offered to buy out the Robbies at a price Huizenga viewed as a good deal, Huizenga would exercise his right of first refusal and buy out the Robbies himself. And since Huizenga was a current owner, he knew more than any third-party buyer could know about the team and the stadium. This would not be a good situation for a third party to step into. A third party would end up owning the Dolphins and the stadium only if it offered too much.

To make matters worse, Huizenga made a public statement to the effect that he would move his baseball team—the Marlins—out of Joe Robbie Stadium if anyone else became an owner of the stadium. One report estimated that, if the Marlins left, the Dolphins and Joe Robbie Stadium would lose about $20 million in value.[4] Thus, the Dolphins and the stadium were worth more to Huizenga than to a third party.

In the end, an outside party made a low bid, and Huizenga exercised his right of first refusal. A colleague of Huizenga's was quoted as saying that the right of first refusal was "the most important thing we did in that negotiation" for Huizenga's investment—adding that "we don't negotiate those things for our health."[5]

8

CODIFYING THE DEAL

Economic analysis of contracts often begins with the theoretical ideal of a *complete, state-contingent contract*. This is a contract that unambiguously assigns obligations to each party under all possible states of the world, and that will be enforced costlessly (or equivalently, that will need no enforcement). The economic analysis in this book has shown ways in which actual contracts must fall short of this ideal. If ex ante information is imperfect, parties will not be able to foresee future contingencies; if ex post information about performance is imperfect, they will not be able to enforce all acts of noncompliance. Another barrier presented by the real world, except in the case of the simplest of contracts, is the inability of parties to think of all details of performance and all future contingencies when they draft a contract—and the practical consideration that, even if they could, it would not be worth the tremendous effort required.

Specifying performance even in reasonably likely scenarios is often not easy. The details can get complicated and require complex negotiation and drafting. But there are alternatives available to parties that want to codify a deal that will keep them working together. One is to use general terms—*standards*, as opposed to specific *rules* aimed at directing precise actions the parties want of each other.[1] In between standards and rules, another possibility is to specify performance that is merely good enough using *simplified rules*. And a last alternative, discussed in Chapter 4, is to create incentives that keep parties working together, rather than try to direct their performance through contractual mandate. Since incentives have already been addressed in Chapter 4, we devote the discussion here to the alternatives of rules, standards, and simplified rules, before closing on the topic of strategic omissions.

Rules

In drafting and negotiating contractual rules and standards, lawyers and their clients make decisions by instinct or experience. But even for experienced lawyers it can be useful to step back and consider what is at stake in the decision to use a rule or a standard or a combination of both. The benefit of a rule is clear. Assuming that a rule specifies precisely the performance a contracting party expects, and that performance is observable and verifiable, enforcement will be relatively certain. The party that is promised performance will either receive it or be compensated for the failure to perform.

But if the benefit of a rule is clear, so too is the cost. In a business deal of any size and complexity, it is difficult for contracting parties to foresee most, let alone all, contingencies and details of performance. Attempting to do so entails costs in terms of parties' and lawyers' time, and it may delay the transaction. Another problem with a rule is that changes in circumstances can expose gaps in the contract. If a scenario is not explicitly covered, no performance is specified and none needs to occur. The specificity that makes a rule desirable can also make it easy to avoid when one party has an incentive to avoid it.

Consider the deal struck between Marvel Studios, a subsidiary of the Walt Disney Company, and the actress Scarlett Johansson after director Jon Favreau offered her the starring role in *Black Widow*. Signed in May 2017, Marvel agreed to a "wide theatrical release" for the film, with Ms. Johansson set to receive the bulk of her compensation in a share of the box office receipts. "Wide theatrical release" was defined in the contract to mean "no less than 1,500 screens."[2] At the time, Disney and other major studios released major films exclusively in theaters and later released them to streaming services, cable TV, DVDs, and other media. A typical theatrical release would run for between 90 and 120 days.

About two years after signing the agreement, filming of *Black Widow* had wrapped and the film was in post-production when, in November 2019, Disney launched a wholly-owned streaming service called Disney+. The Johansson contract was silent with respect to showing the movie on Disney+, since the service had not existed when the contract was negotiated. Then, in early 2020, COVID-19 struck, and theaters closed. The release of *Black Widow* was pushed back a full year, to July 9, 2021. Yet even after a year, theaters were relatively empty. So, on that date, Disney released the movie in theaters, but simultaneously made it available to stream on Disney+ for $30—a scenario the parties had not contemplated when they negotiated the contract.

Ms. Johansson sued Disney, claiming that the simultaneous release on Disney+ was a breach of Disney's commitment to a wide theatrical release. She argued that both parties had "understood this meant that the movie would initially be released *exclusively in movie theatres,* and that it would remain *exclusively in movie theatres* for a period of between approximately 90 and 120 days."[3] Ms. Johansson claimed a loss of millions of dollars in potential box office proceeds as the Disney+ streaming diverted what would have been box office sales. Disney responded that there was "no merit whatsoever to this filing."[4] The parties settled quickly, on undisclosed terms.

We will never know how a court would have interpreted "wide theatrical release" in this dispute. But, the terms seem clear, and they do not say "wide theatrical release prior to a digital release." Of course, Disney violated the spirit of the deal, and a court might have interpreted the contract in Johansson's favor. But a court could well have concluded that a rule is a rule, and that Disney did not violate the rule the parties had negotiated. This case shows how an unforeseen change in circumstances can create a gap in a contract that creates an opportunity for exploitation. When a scenario is not explicitly covered, no performance is specified for that scenario, and none needs to occur.

Standards

An alternative to a rule is a standard: rather than specifying performance in detail, parties can agree to a broad statement of what they expect from each other. In a supply agreement, it is common for parties to provide, for example, that the supplier will deliver a product of "merchantable quality," rather than setting out detailed specifications for its product. More generally, parties might agree that performance of a contract will be "commercially reasonable," or that one or both will exert "reasonable effort." We saw this in the SemiCo-TestCo deal in Chapter 7.

Not all terms of all deals can be codified with standards. It would be unrealistic for Scarlett Johansson and Marvel simply to agree that Johansson would be paid "reasonable compensation." But in many situations standards can be used appropriately. If a deal unfolds as expected, there will be no disagreement regarding fulfillment of a standard and the parties will certainly have gained by saving themselves the trouble of specifying all the details. If circumstances change, a standard can allow for adaptation and an alignment of expectations better than a rule would. But it also might not. Standards leave the details for later and, if the parties do not agree with how those details are filled in, a judge may have to decide for them. Standards thus provide flexibility to meet changing circumstances, but also create uncertainty regarding how a deal will play out under different scenarios and how a judge might interpret a party's broadly phrased commitment if there is a dispute.

Combining Rules and Standards

The disadvantage of a rule, then, is that it may leave gaps, especially if circumstances change, while the disadvantage of a standard is its vagueness and associated uncertainty. One way to minimize these disadvantages—and exploit the advantages each has to offer—is to combine the two by backing up a rule with a standard that will fill gaps the rule may leave open.

Merger and acquisition agreements take this approach. Consider the Microsoft-LinkedIn acquisition agreement discussed in previous chapters. As is generally true of acquirors, between the time the parties signed the agreement and the time the deal would close, Microsoft wanted LinkedIn's managers to keep the company running as it had been before they agreed to sell it. An *ordinary course* obligation helped to achieve this:

> [T]he Company [LinkedIn] will, and will cause each of its Subsidiaries to . . . conduct its business and operations *in the ordinary course* of business; and (iii) use its *respective reasonable best efforts* to (A) preserve intact its material assets, properties, Contracts or other legally binding understandings, licenses and business organizations; (B) keep available the services of its current officers and key employees; and (C) preserve the current relationships and goodwill with customers, suppliers, distributors, lessors, licensors, licensees, creditors, contractors and other Persons with which the Company or any of its Subsidiaries has business relations.[5]

In short, LinkedIn's core obligation was to conduct its business "in the ordinary course of business" and use "reasonable best efforts" to keep its business intact. These are deliberately vague standards.

"Reasonable best efforts" is not only vague but almost incoherent—what does it mean for efforts to be "best" and also "reasonable"? Nevertheless, this is a commonly used "efforts" standard.

These standards did not tell LinkedIn precisely how it should preserve its assets, employees, and customers—nor could the parties ever specify such a set of rules. Each party's hope was that, with the benefit of hindsight, if there were a dispute, a court would apply the "ordinary course" and "reasonable best efforts" standards in a way that fit that party's expectations. If Microsoft relied solely on these standards, it would be subject to uncertainty regarding LinkedIn's condition at closing. If circumstances arose for which there was no precedent to anchor the "ordinary course" obligation, such as the COVID-19 pandemic, LinkedIn and Microsoft could disagree regarding how LinkedIn should be managed, and it was anyone's guess how a court would resolve a dispute.

But Microsoft and LinkedIn, like all parties to merger or acquisition agreements, chose not to rely solely on these standards. They also agreed to a long list of covenants written as specific rules that would govern LinkedIn's operations between the time of signing and closing. For example, subject to certain qualifications, LinkedIn agreed not to:

- "propose or adopt a plan of complete or partial liquidation, dissolution, merger, consolidation, restructuring, recapitalization or other reorganization";
- "directly or indirectly acquire, repurchase or redeem any securities";
- "acquire (by merger, consolidation or acquisition of stock or assets or otherwise), or make any investment in any interest in, any assets or any other [company] or any equity interest therein, except for purchases of assets in the ordinary course of business";
- "sell or otherwise dispose of (whether by merger, consolidation or disposition of stock or assets or otherwise) any assets constituting a material line of business";

- "incur, assume, suffer or modify the terms of any Indebtedness";
- "enter into, adopt, amend (including accelerating the vesting), modify or terminate any employee compensation plan"; or
- "settle, release, waive or compromise any pending or threatened [legal proceeding]."[6]

These rules, among others, were clear statements that prevented LinkedIn from taking certain actions—actions which were probably already covered by the reasonable best efforts and ordinary course standards, but regarding which, because these were rules, there would be absolutely no doubt. Gaps surely remained, but the combination of the list of rules with the ordinary course and reasonable best efforts standards covered a lot of what might otherwise go wrong between signing and closing.

Simplified Rules

An alternative to a rule or a standard is a *simplified rule*. This is a contract term that the parties know is imperfect, perhaps substantially imperfect. The virtue of a simplified rule is that, like any rule, it leaves little if any room for dispute regarding what the contract requires. It may put one or the other party in a position it regrets, but that is a possibility the parties are willing to tolerate to avoid both the time-consuming negotiating and drafting associated with a complex, well-tailored rule and the uncertainty and potentially costly litigation associated with a standard.

Commercial loan agreements often use simplified rules to constrain the borrower's conduct while the loan is outstanding. For example, borrowers typically agree not to incur any debt that would be senior to the loan, or any *pari-passu* debt (which would put another lender on equal footing to it) over a certain amount. They also agree that they will not, during the period of the loan, enter into a new line of business. Neither of these rules is precisely what either party wants. Surely if taking on additional debt would allow the borrower to purchase assets or expand its business in a way that would reduce risk to the lender, the lender would want to allow that new borrowing. The same would be true if the borrower entered into a new, profitable, and low-risk line of business. The lender's real concern is that the borrower not increase its risk of default. But it is difficult to write a rule into a loan agreement that prevents new debt or a new business *only* if it increases risk to the lender. For many circumstances, the simplified rule will be good enough.

Moreover, a simplified rule need not leave the parties in a sub-optimal position, with their hands tied, as circumstances arise. If a borrower wants to enter a lucrative new line of business that does not increase its risk of defaulting on its loan, it can always ask the lender to allow it to do so. Even if the risk of default will increase, the borrower and lender can renegotiate the loan with a higher interest rate or a change in other terms.

If from the outset, however, a party expects that it will likely ask its counterparty to renegotiate a simplified rule, it may want to write that possibility into its agreement. Suppose a borrower is aware of several new lines of business that it might want to enter while a loan is outstanding. The idea of going to the lender every time to get permission is unappealing. Even worse, to get the lender's consent, the borrower will need to tell the lender how lucrative the lines of business will be, which will give the lender leverage to extract additional terms in exchange for granting permission. This is a case where the simplified rule won't work. The borrower should push for a more tailored rule—for example, specifying certain lines of business for which it will not have to seek approval. Alternatively, if the exceptions are too difficult to enumerate, the borrower and lender can specify a process by which the lender will consent to exceptions from the simplified rule. The lender might also agree that it will consider requests for exceptions in good faith. This combines a simplified rule with a standard. Like other standards, good faith can be ambiguous in particular settings, but it generally refers to honest intentions and commercial reasonability.[7]

Strategic Omissions

There is one last alternative to rules, standards, and simplified rules. Parties may deliberately leave a contractual issue unresolved. This can happen when there is a contingency that is not central to the deal, or that is unlikely to occur, and at least one side fears that agreement could not be reached on the particular point if it were raised. In this scenario, they might choose not to risk the overall deal for a less important or less likely contingency.

Back to the *Black Widow* contract, some commentators wondered why the parties did not get more specific about what a "wide theatrical release" meant—and in particular, why the parties did not specify that a wide theatrical release meant a release before streaming. Direct-to-home streaming was certainly known in May 2017, even if COVID was not, and even if Disney+ had not yet launched. Ms. Johansson's attorneys claimed that both parties "understood this meant that the Picture would initially be released *exclusively in movie theatres,* and that it would remain *exclusively in movie theatres* for a period of between approximately 90 and 120 days."[8] But if "both parties" understood this, why was their understanding not documented in the contract?

The answer might be *strategic omission,* a choice not to include a term on which the parties would likely not be able to agree (in this case, on precisely what they meant by a "wide theatrical release"). If caused to consider the scenario in the negotiating process, Ms. Johansson's attorneys would likely have pushed for longer exclusivity in theaters (for example, at least 120 days) while Disney's attorneys would likely have wanted shorter guaranteed exclusivity in theaters to give them more flexibility—particularly if they were aware at the time of the possibility of Disney+. The result might have been an impasse on what was at the time a relatively minor issue. Moreover, at the time they negotiated their deal, both parties wanted to maximize the revenues from a "wide theatrical release," so they might have thought it better to rely on aligned incentives, rather than fight about how to define "wide theatrical release."

Commenting on the *Black Widow* litigation, a legal editor for the *Hollywood Reporter* observed that "not every point in an actor's contract is negotiated to its zenith. A lot of shorthand is used, and the parties accept a great deal of ambiguity almost by design." Putting a finer point on "by design," the piece goes on to quote a veteran talent lawyer: "If you're going to ask for something, better be sure you'll get it. Often, the smart ones conclude it's in the best interest to not raise the issue. The last thing you wish to create is clarity that you don't have what you wanted."[9]

Notes

1. THE BASIC NEGOTIATION MODEL AND BARGAINING POWER

1. Robert H. Mnookin, Scott R. Peppet, and Andrew S. Tulumello, *Beyond Winning: Negotiating to Create Value in Deals and Disputes* (Cambridge, MA: Belknap Press of Harvard University Press, 2000), 19–22.

2. Thomas Schelling, *The Strategy of Conflict,* with new preface (Cambridge, MA: Harvard University Press, 1981), 22, 24.

3. Howard Raiffa, John Richardson, and David Metcalfe, *Negotiation Analysis: The Science and Art of Collaborative Decision-Making* (Cambridge, MA: Harvard University Press, 2002).

4. G. Richard Shell, Bargaining for Advantage: Bargaining for Advantage: Negotiation Strategies for Reasonable People, 2nd ed. (New York, Penguin, 2006).

5. G. Richard Shell, *Bargaining for Advantage: Negotiation Strategies for Reasonable People,* 2nd ed. (New York: Penguin, 2006).

2. EX ANTE INFORMATION CHALLENGES

1. Kenneth J. Arrow, "Uncertainty and the Welfare Economics of Medical Care," *The American Economic Review* 53 (1963): 941–973; George A. Akerlof, "The Market for 'Lemons': Quality Uncertainty and the Market Mechanism," *Quarterly Journal of Economics* 84 (1970): 488–500; Michael Rothschild and Joseph Stiglitz, "Equilibrium in Competitive Insurance Markets: An Essay on the Economics of Imperfect Information," *Quarterly Journal of Economics* 90 (1976): 629–649.

2. Akerlof, "The Market for 'Lemons,'" 488–500.

3. Lee Ross, "Reactive Devaluation in Negotiation and Conflict Resolution," in *Barriers to Conflict Resolution,* ed. Kenneth Arrow, Robert Mnookin, Lee Ross, Amos Tversky, and Robert B. Wilson (New York: W. W. Norton, 1995).

4. The film is a dramatization of a book by the same name by Jonathan Harr (New York: Random House, 1995) telling the story of the real-life case of *Anne Anderson, et al., v. Cryovac, Inc., et al.,* in which residents of Woburn, MA, in 1986, sued corporations for groundwater contamination. *A Civil Action,* Steven Zaillian, director and writer (Walt Disney / Touchstone, 1998).

5. This story is based loosely on William A. Sahlman, "Business Research Corp. (A)," Harvard Business School Case Study 9-285-089.

6. Michael Spence provided the first model of signaling. A. M. Spence, *Market Signaling: Information Transfer in Hiring and Related Processes* (Cambridge, MA: Harvard University Press, 1973).

7. Grossman was the first to model seller disclosure and warranties in the product market context. Sanford J. Grossman, "The Informational Role of Warranties and Private Disclosure about Product Quality," *Journal of Law and Economics* 24, no. 3 (1981): 461–483.

8. The agreement between Fresenius and Akorn qualified the regulatory compliance representation by providing that Akorn would be in breach only if the falsity of the representation caused its business (the target of the acquisition) to suffer a "material adverse effect"—that is, in the Delaware court's interpretation of the phrase, if it "substantially threaten[ed] the overall earnings potential of the target in a durationally-significant manner." *In Re IBP, Inc. Shareholders Litigation v. Tyson Foods,* 789 A.2d 14 (Del. Ch. 2001). The court held that Akorn's noncompliance met this definition. *Akorn, Inc. v. Fresenius Kabi AG,* C. A. No. 2018-0300-JTL (Del. Ch. 2018). One of us (Subramanian) served as an expert witness for Akorn, presenting empirical evidence on a separate requirement that Akorn act in the "ordinary course of business" between signing and closing.

9. *Mattei v. Hopper,* 51 Cal. 2d 119 (1958). This analysis tracks Victor Goldberg, *Framing Contract Law: An Economic Perspective* (Cambridge, MA: Harvard University Press, 2006). See Chapter 4: "Satisfaction Clauses: Consideration without Good Faith," 91–98.

10. Victor P. Goldberg, "The Gold Ring Problem," *University of Toronto Law Journal* 47 (1997): 469–494; Guhan Subramanian, *Dealmaking: The New Strategy of Negotiauctions*, 2nd ed. (New York: W. W. Norton, 2020).

11. Subramanian, *Dealmaking*.

12. Ronald J. Gilson, "Value Creation by Business Lawyers: Legal Skills and Asset Pricing," *Yale Law Journal* 94, no. 2 (1984): 239–313, 253.

13. *Akorn v. Fresenius Kabi*, 2018 WL 4719347 (2018)

14. One of us (Subramanian) served as an advisor and potential expert witness for LVMH.

3. BRIDGING VALUATION GAPS WITH EARNOUTS

1. For studies focused on the use of earnouts to respond to asymmetric information, see Albert H. Choi, "Facilitating Mergers and Acquisitions with Earnouts and Purchase Price Adjustments," *Journal of Law, Finance and Accounting* 2, no. 1 (2017): 1–47; Matthew D. Cain, David J. Denis, and Diane K. Denis, "Earnouts: A Study of Financial Contracting in Acquisition Agreements," *Journal of Accounting and Economics* 51 (2011): 151–170; Srikant Datar, Richard Frankel, and Mark Wolfson, "Earnouts: The Effects of Adverse Selection and Agency Costs on Acquisition Techniques," *Journal of Law, Economics & Organization* 17 (2008): 201–238; Ninon Kohers and James Ang, "Earnouts in Mergers: Agreeing to Disagree and Agreeing to Stay," *Journal of Business* 73, no. 3 (2000): 445–476; Roberto Ragozzino and Jeffrey J. Reuer, "Contingent Earnouts in Acquisitions of Privately-Held Targets," *Journal of Management* 35 (2009): 857–879. For a study concluding that, on average, earnouts are used in situations of symmetric uncertainty, see Brian J. M. Quinn, "Putting Your Money Where Your Mouth Is: The Performance of Earnouts in Corporate Acquisitions," *University of Cincinnati Law Review* 81 (2013): 127–172.

2. "Wipro acquires US-based cMango for $20mn," *Business Standard,* January 19, 2013, https://www.business-standard.com/article/technology/wipro-acquires-us-based-cmango-for-20mn-106022000044_1.html.

3. Max H. Bazerman and J. J. Gillespie, "Betting on the Future: The Virtues of Contingent Contracts," *Harvard Business Review,* September–October 1999, 155–160.

4. See Choi, "Facilitating Mergers and Acquisitions"; Albert Choi, "Addressing Informational Challenges with Earnouts in Mergers and Acquisitions," in *Research Handbook on Mergers and Acquisitions,* ed. Claire Hill and Steven Davidoff Solomon (Northampton, MA: Edward Elgar Press, 2016).

5. Shira Ovide, "The Benefits of Deal 'Schmuck Insurance,'" *Wall Street Journal,* June 13, 2011.

6. One of us (Subramanian) joined the board of LKQ shortly after this deal closed.

7. SRS Acquiom Inc., "2021 SRS Acquiom Life Sciences M&A Study," 13, https://info.srsacquiom.com/2021-life-sciences-study. For more on deals outside the life sciences sector, see SRS Acquiom Inc., "2022 SRS Acquiom, 2022 M&A Deal Terms Study," May 10, 2022, https://www.srsacquiom.com/resources/m-a-deal-terms-study/.

8. SRS Acquiom reports that in 2021, just 16 percent of earnouts used earnings as a metric at least in part, while 66 percent used revenues and 39 percent used something else, such as unit sales or product launches. SRS Acquiom Inc., "2022 M&A Deal Terms Study," chart on 24.

9. *Sonoran Scanners v. PerkinElmer,* 590 F. Supp. 196, 209 (2008).

10. *LaPoint v. Amerisourcebergen,* 2007 WL 2565709 (2007).

11. *LaPoint v. Amerisourcebergen,* 2007 WL 2565709 (2007), at *9.

12. For a description of CVRs, see Igor Kirman and Victor Goldfeld, "Contingent Value Rights (CVRs)," *Practical Law,* Thomson Reuters, https://www.wlrk.com/webdocs/wlrknew/AttorneyPubs/WLRK.26465.19.pdf.

13. Stephen D. Simpson, "For Forest Labs, Inc, Deals Are Coming Fast and Furiex," *Motley Fool,* April 28, 2014, https://www.fool.com/investing/general/2014/04/28/for-forest-labs-inc-deals-are-coming-fast-and-furi.aspx.

14. These details of the Contingent Value Rights Agreement are noted in Item 1.01 of Forest Laboratories, Inc.'s Form 8-K, filed April 27, 2014, with the United States Securities and Exchange Commission, https://www.sec.gov/Archives/edgar/data/38074/000119312514163514/d717084d8k.htm. The CVR Agreement itself is included as Annex C to Furiex's Proxy Statement dated June 4, 2014, https://www.sec.gov/Archives/edgar/data/1484478/000119312514225775/d727381ddefm14a.htm#toc727381_78.

4. MORAL HAZARD AND INCENTIVE DESIGN

1. Paul Milgrom and John Roberts, *Economics, Organization and Management* (New York: Prentice Hall 1992), ch. 6, 167–168. Non-economists (including lawyers) often use the term *moral hazard* more broadly and incorrectly, to refer to distortions in behavior due to the contract, regardless of whether actions are observable or verifiable.

2. The two can coincide where, for example, a party knows it is not the type that works hard in the absence of strong incentives.

3. Tom Baker, "On the Genealogy of Moral Hazard," *Texas Law Review* 75 (1996): 237–292; David Rowell and Luke B. Connelly, "A History of the Term Moral Hazard," *The Journal of Risk and Insurance* 79 (2021): 1051–1075.

4. Mark Pauly, "The Economics of Moral Hazard," *American Economic Review* 58 (1968): 31–58; Kenneth Arrow, "Uncertainty and the Welfare Economics of Medical Care," *American Economic Review* 53 (1963): 941–973.

5. Bengt Holmström, "Moral Hazard and Observability," *Bell Journal of Economics* 10, no. 1 (1979): 74–91. For a summary of the literature, see Canice Prendergast, "The Provision of Incentives in Firms," *Journal of Economic Literature* 37, no. 7 (1999): 7–63; Milgrom and Roberts, *Economics, Organization and Management*, ch. 7.

6. The tradeoff between risk-bearing and incentives is discussed in Milgrom and Roberts, *Economics, Organization and Management*, chs. 6 and 7.

7. Prendergast, "The Provision of Incentives in Firms," 7, 21.

8. Bengt Holmstrom and Paul Milgrom, "Multitask Principal–Agent Analyses: Incentive Contracts, Asset Ownership and Job Design," *Journal of Law, Economics, and Organization* 7, no. 24 (1991): 24–52.

9. Prendergast, "The Provision of Incentives in Firms," 21.

10. See Michael Klausner and Stephen Venuto, "Liquidation Rights and Incentive Misalignment in Start-Up Financing," *Cornell Law Review* 98, no. 6 (2013): 1399–1435.

11. For a complete analysis of the dysfunctionality of SPACs, only some of which is covered here, see Michael Klausner, Michael Ohlrogge, and Emily Ruan, "A Sober Look at SPACs," *Yale Journal on Regulation* 39 (2022): 228–303.

12. This is explained in detail in Klausner, Ohlrogge, and Ruan, "A Sober Look at SPACs."

13. Klausner, Ohlrogge, and Ruan, "A Sober Look at SPACs," 228.

14. In motions to dismiss, the Delaware Court of Chancery has ruled in favor of shareholders in three cases alleging a failure to disclose the amount of cash underlying SPAC shares. *In Re XL Fleet (Pivotal) Stockholder Litigation*, Delaware Court of Chancery, June 9, 2023; *Laidlaw v. GigAcquisitions2*, Delaware Court of Chancery, March 1, 2023; *Delman v. GigAcquisitions3*, Delaware Court of Chancery, January 4, 2023. One of us (Klausner) is co-counsel in these cases and others.

15. On the defendants' motion to dismiss the case, the court ruled in the plaintiffs' favor. *Delman v. GigAcquisitions3*, Delaware Court of Chancery, January 4, 2023. One of us (Klausner) is co-counsel representing the class of SPAC shareholders in this case.

5. ASSET SPECIFICITY AND LONG-TERM CONTRACTS

1. Oliver E. Williamson, "Credible Commitments: Using Hostages to Support Exchange," *American Economic Review* 73, no. 4 (1983): 519–540.

2. While others would go on to refine it further, the concept of asset specificity was initially developed by Oliver Williamson. Oliver E. Williamson, *Markets and Hierarchies: Analysis and Antitrust Implications* (New York: Free Press, 1975); Oliver E. Williamson, *The Economic Institutions of Capitalism* (New York: Free Press, 1985); Williamson, "Credible Commitments,"; Oliver E. Williamson, *Economic Organization: Firms, Markets, and Policy Control* (New York: New York University Press, 1986).

3. This concept was developed by Oliver Hart and John Moore. Oliver Hart and John Moore, "Contracts as Reference Points," *The Quarterly Journal of Economics* 123, no. 1 (2008): 1–48; Hart, "Hold-Up, Asset Ownership, and Reference Points," *The Quarterly Journal of Economics* 124, no. 1 (2009): 267–300.

4. Oliver Williamson, *The Economic Institutions of Capitalism* (New York: Free Press, 1985), 95.

5. Benjamin Klein, Robert G. Crawford, and Armen A. Alchian, "Vertical Integration, Appropriable Rents and the Competitive Contracting Process," *Journal of Law and Economics* 21, no. 2 (1978): 297–326, 308–314.

6. For additional work developing these concepts, see Victor P. Goldberg, "Regulation and Administered Contracts," *Bell Journal of Eco-*

nomics 7, no. 2 (1976): 426–448, 439–441; Victor P. Goldberg. "Relational Exchange: Economics and Complex Contracts," *American Behavioral Scientist* 23, no. 3 (1980): 337–352; Klein, Crawford, and Alchian, "Vertical Integration, Appropriable Rents, and the Competitive Contracting Process," 308–314.

7. R. H Coase, "The Nature of the Firm: Origin, Meaning, Influence," *Journal of Law, Economics, and Organization* 4 (1988), 337–352.

8. See, for example, Paul L. Joskow, "Contract Duration and Relationship-Specific Investments: Empirical Evidence from Coal Markets," *American Economic Review* 77, no. 1 (1987): 168–185.

9. See also J. Harold Mulhern, "Complexity in Long-Term Contracts: An Analysis of Natural Gas Contractual Provision," *Journal of Law, Economics and Organization* 2 (1986): 105–118.

10. Victor P. Goldberg and John R. Erickson, "Quantity and Price Adjustment in Long-Term Contracts: A Case Study of Petroleum Coke," *Journal of Law and Economics* 30, no. 2 (1987): 369–398; Victor Goldberg, *Framing Contract Law: An Economic Perspective* (Cambridge, MA: Harvard University Press, 2006), 104–106.

11. Benjamin Klein and Keith B. Leffler, "The Role of Market Forces in Assuring Contractual Performance," *Journal of Political Economy* 89, no. 4 (1981): 615–641.

12. Stewart Macauley, "Non-Contractual Relations in Business: A Preliminary Study," *American Sociological Review* 28, no. 1 (1963): 55–67.

13. Klein, Crawford, and Alchian, "Vertical Integration, Appropriable Rents, and the Competitive Contracting Process," 303.

6. QUANTITY AND PRICE ADJUSTMENT IN LONG-TERM CONTRACTS

1. Victor Goldberg and John Erickson, "Quantity and Price Adjustment in Long-Term Contracts: A Case Study of Petroleum Coke," *Journal of Law and Economics* 30 (1987): 369–398.

2. Utpal Dholakia, "When Cost-Plus Pricing is a Good Idea," July 12, 2018, https://hbr.org/2018/07/when-cost-plus-pricing-is-a-good-idea.

3. This discussion of the Essex-Alcoa transaction is based on Goldberg, "Price Adjustment in Long-Term Contracts," 527, 530; and Goldberg, *Framing Contract Law,* ch. 20, "Alcoa v. Essex, Anatomy of a Bungled Deal."

7. EXITING A LONG-TERM DEAL

1. One of us (Subramanian) was an expert witness in the Delaware Chancery Court litigation over which process would be used.

2. One of us (Subramanian) provided expert testimony for Carlyle, making the point that an obligation to "consider in good faith" is a minimal obligation at best.

3. We are omitting a twist in this particular buy-sell whereby an offer by Levi's to buy out Designs was subject to a "minimum value" limit. The mechanics of the provision did not work to protect Designs.

4. David Satterfield and Scott Fowler, "Robbies Agree to Sell Dolphins, Sources Say," *Miami Herald,* June 15, 1993, 1A.

5. Jeff Snook, "Huizenga Awaiting Letter of Intent on Robbies' Deal," *Palm Beach Post,* June 17, 1993, 1C. For more on this deal, see Anthony Faiola, "Huizenga Wants Stadium, Not Dolphins: Concern Is to Protect Marlins," *Miami Herald,* July 1, 1993, at C1, C3; S. L. Price, "Huizenga Dances around Dolphins Sale," *Miami Herald,* June 16, 1993, 8B–9B; Gail DeGeorge, *The Making of a Blockbuster: How Wayne Huizenga Built a Sports and Entertainment Empire from Trash, Grit, and Videotape* (New York: Wiley, 1995), 218, 245.

8. CODIFYING THE DEAL

1. Two classic articles examining the difference between rules and standards are Louis Kaplow, "Rules versus Standards: An Economic Analysis," *Duke Law Journal* 42 (1992): 557–629; and Robert E. Scott and George G. Triantis, "Anticipating Litigation in Contract Design," *Yale Law Journal* 115 (2006): 814–879.

2. Complaint in *Periwinkle Entertainment, Inc., F/S/O Scarlett Johansson, v. The Walt Disney Co.,* Case No 21STCV27831 (Cal. 2021), 8.

3. *Periwinkle Entertainment, Inc., F/S/O Scarlett Johansson, v. The Walt Disney Co.,* Case No. 21STCV27831 (Cal. 2021), 8.

4. "Disney Says 'No Merit' to Scarlett Johansson Lawsuit over 'Black Widow' Movie," Reuters, July 29, 2021.

5. Microsoft-LinkedIn Acquisition Agreement, Section 5.1. https://www .sec.gov/Archives/edgar/data/1271024/000110465916130837/a16-14187 _1prem14a.htm#AnnexA_075209.

6. Microsoft-LinkedIn Acquisition Agreement.

7. Former United States Supreme Court Justice Souter, when he was a justice on the New Hampshire Supreme Court, provided an analysis of case law applying the good faith concept. *Centronics Corp. v. Genicom Corp.* 562 A.2d 187, 190–195 (New Hampshire Supreme Court 1989).

8. Complaint in *Periwinkle Entertainment, Inc., F/S/O Scarlett Johansson, v. The Walt Disney Co.,* Case No 21STCV27831 (Cal. 2021), 8.

9. Eriq Gardner, "How the 'Black Widow' Battle Could Break the Mold on Hollywood Dealmaking," *Hollywood Reporter,* August 25, 2021, https://www.hollywoodreporter.com/business/business-news/how -black-widow-battle-could-change-long-standing-industry-customs -1235002215/.

Acknowledgments

There are many people to thank for their contributions. Most notably, we are grateful to Ron Gilson, Victor Goldberg, and Dan Raff for getting it started and for commenting on various case studies over the years. We also thank Rob Daines, George Triantis, Brian Quinn, John Crawford, and Michael Knoll for helpful comments and early drafts of case studies and helpful conversations. Many Stanford Law, Harvard Law, and Harvard Business School students have helped to write the case studies and other course materials that made their way into the book. We hope we do not omit any as we specifically thank John Robinson, John Crawford, Jason Berg, Zachary Fedorko, Ashley Romero, Scott Toussaint, Jun Feng, Spencer Williams, Alan Fishman, Chris Best, Yina Dong, Philip Zeigler, Jessica Park, Omeed Anvar, Elyssa Pak, Marin Babb, Blake Bailey, Beverly Moore, Raaj Narayan, and Brandon Ho. Finally, we acknowledge the work of Guhan's coauthors at Harvard: Professor Julian Zlatev of Harvard Business School and Raseem Farook (HBS '21), who coauthored a case on LVMH's bid for Tiffany; Michelle Kalka, who coauthored the *Frasier* case studies; and Dae (Dan) Kang, HLS '21, who coauthored the case study on Far Point's merger with Global Blue.

Index